A HISTORY OF CANNIBALISM

A HISTORY OF CANNIBALISM

FROM ANCIENT CULTURES TO SURVIVAL STORIES AND MODERN PSYCHOPATHS

Nathan Constantine

CHARTWELL
BOOKS, INC.

This edition printed in 2006 by
CHARTWELL BOOKS, INC.
A Division of **BOOK SALES, INC.**
114 Northfield Avenue
Edison, New Jersey 08837

Copyright © 2006 Arcturus Publishing Limited
26/27 Bickels Yard, 151–153 Bermondsey Street,
London SE1 3HA

ISBN-13: 978-0-7858-2158-8
ISBN-10: 0-7858-2158-9

Printed in China

Contents

Introduction

At first glance, cannibalism seems easy to define: the 'practice of eating one's own kind' as *The Penguin English Dictionary* succinctly puts it. That seems straightforward enough, but it begs any number of questions and glosses over a remarkable diversity. Chewing on a human liver seems unambiguously cannibalistic, but does the chewing of fingernail chunks qualify nail-biters as cannibals? What, essentially, is the difference?

Because it is so hard to pin down, and so often a question of context and circumstance, cannibalism comes in degrees of acceptability. At one extreme the chewed fingernail, at the other sadistic murder, mutilation and the roasting of flesh. In between these two extremes lie a multitude of possibilities. In ethical terms, it clearly makes a huge difference whether the source of meat is alive or dead. If the former, it obviously matters whether the donor was willing or not; if the latter, whether the would-be consumer was also the cause of death.

These days we tend to take the simple line. Everything is good or evil, and cannibalism clearly falls into the latter category. When a few poor souls find themselves trapped in the middle of

nowhere without any food, and end up having to eat their companions, most of us agree they had no choice, and generously forgive their fall from grace, because we still believe that that is what it was – a horrible necessity. But we still hold on to its wrongness; cannibalism is quite simply, and innately, unacceptable.

So why do people do it? Why – since we are generally incapable of imagining a world very different from our own – have people ever done it? There are three essential reasons: duty, desperation and desire. Or, put another way, because they ought to, need to or want to. This book is divided accordingly, though there is obviously an element of overlap – many individuals and peoples have had more than one motive for eating their own. The Maoris, for example, found cannibalism both socially acceptable and necessary, and they also seemed to enjoy it. And when it comes to psychopathic behaviour, the line between needs and wants gets more than a little blurry.

Desperation and desire

Desperation cannibalism is easy enough to understand. There have been famines throughout history, on every continent, in areas of every size, from the wide Russian Steppes to narrow lifeboats in mid-ocean. Some of these famines have had natural causes, others have been the direct result of man's activities. The outcome, in any case, has usually been the same. Desperate

There are three essential reasons [for cannibalism]: duty, desperation and desire.

Goya's *Cronus Eating His Children*, illustrating a story from Greek mythology, highlights the enduring fascination Europeans have had with the idea of cannibalism throughout history

people do desperate things, and hungry people eat what they can, even if it is other people.

Desire cannibalism is much harder to understand, though abusive fathers, overbearing mothers, animal torture and extreme sexual dysfunction all seem to crop up rather frequently by way of a possible explanation for it. Humanity's history – humanity's present, come to that – contains groups who practise it culturally, but desire cannibalism in the modern world is largely the province of individuals, a family affair at most. Since society assumes that cannibalism is utterly wrong, and that those so inclined should be capable of restraining themselves, it follows that those who do not are the ultimate outsiders, people who give ordinary murderers a bad name. Few cannibal-killers have been found to be insane, but only because most juries have been so shocked by their actions that they have been all too eager to execute them.

c. 1505: A European sailing ship sails warily towards the shores of the New World. The Caribs gave their name to 'cannibalism'

The way things were

But first, duty or cultural cannibalism. By this, we do not mean one that demands that everyone eats as much human flesh as they can manage because it is the 'done thing' to do. Duty cannibalism arises from a shared belief in many societies that eating other people actually helps their world go round, their culture cohere.

How, you might ask, could anyone believe anything so weird, so bad, so 'wrong'? Well, those who dismiss such beliefs should look at their own. The world made in six days? The same world saved by a well-stocked boat of animals? All cultures, like all individuals, have their own ways of making sense of things they cannot understand. It is a case of culture, and that culture's beliefs and social mores.

So how might it help to eat other humans? What hopes could be fulfilled? If it is done for the gods they are bound to be grateful; they'll keep the world turning, keep the sun rising, keep the crops growing. And then there is the magic of flesh and blood, and the belief that it must be transferable. It does not take a huge

> **It does not take a huge stretch of the imagination to believe that consuming the flesh of a fearsome enemy would make you stronger...**

stretch of the imagination to believe that consuming the flesh of a fearsome enemy would make you stronger, or that drinking the blood of the healthy might cure disease. So the Ashanti forced their cowards to eat the hearts of the brave, and the Pharaohs bathed in young blood to wash away leprosy; such transfers of corporeal assets carried all sorts of wonderful possibilities.

Simple notions for simple societies, you might think. Sixteenth-century France was much more sophisticated. 'Tie a naked, red-haired, male Catholic to a bench', one, presumably Anglican, medicinal recipe begins, 'and subject him to the unrestrained attentions of a number of venomous animals. When he has expired from the bites and stings, hang him upside-down with a bowl underneath to catch the drips. Mix these with the fat of a man who has been hanged, the entrails of children, and the corpses of the venomous animals who caused his death. Use as required' (see Askenasy, Bibliography).

Cook had several Tahitians on his ship, and they made their abhorrance of cannibalism clear to the Maoris.

It was not just a matter of transference. Eating an enemy was a good way of punishing him, a satisfyingly complete form of revenge, a dramatic deterrent to others. And it was not just a matter of enemies. Eating dead relatives could save them from the loneliness of burial, and put a limit to the living's period of grief.

Dietary and economic factors also came into play. In some places, human flesh might be the only available source of protein. In others, it might provide the community's main source of income, and if this was the case then chances were good that the practice would be considered morally acceptable. How many times have we heard politicians say that cutting back the arms trade would put too many jobs at risk?

For these reasons and more, many more cultures than not have woven the practice of cannibalism into their daily lives.

And why not?

One last thought. It is all very well asking 'Why cannibalism?' For most of history the more pertinent question has been 'Why not?'

In the first decade of the twentieth century, J.H.P. Murray was Lieutenant-Governor and Chief Judicial Officer of Anglo-Australian Papua New Guinea. In his memoirs he remembered a trial

witness's matter-of-fact description of his tribe's cannibalistic practices: 'We boil the bodies. We cut them up and boil them in a pot. We boil babies too. We cut them up like a pig. We eat them hot or cold. We eat the legs first. We eat them because they are like fish. We have fish in the creeks, and kangaroos in the grass. But men are our real food' (see Hogg, Bibliography).

Murray obviously thought about this and other statements he heard during his time in Papua New Guinea. The idea revolted him, but he searched in vain for a convincing reason why. 'Certain tribes here like human flesh', he wrote later, 'and do not see why they should not eat it. Indeed, I have never been able to give a convincing answer to a native who says to me, "Why should I not eat human flesh?"' (see Hogg, Bibliography).

The famous Victorian traveller Alfred St Johnston went even further. 'I should have gloried in the rush and struggle of old Fijian times', he wrote in 1883, 'with my hand against everybody, and everybody against me; and the fierce madness of unchecked passion and rage with which they went to battle, and the clubbing of my foes. And – I am sure I should have enjoyed the eating of them afterwards' (see St Johnston, Bibliography).

If stiff-necked Victorian colonials found it hard to say why not, and red-misted Victorian explorers were all for joining in, small wonder that the colonized and explored asked what all the fuss was about. As a group of Maoris told Captain Cook: 'Can there be any harm in eating our enemies, whom we have killed in

The warlike Maoris consumed their enemies as part of their right as winners of the battle

battle? Would not those very enemies have done the same to us?' Cook had several Tahitians on his ship, and they made their abhorrence of cannibalism clear to the Maoris. The latter, Cook reported, 'only laughed at them' (see Hogg, Bibliography).

They were still laughing fifty years later. The French doctor, Felix Maynard, recounted one Maori chief's patient explanation to his dim foreign guest, of how fish ate fish, dogs ate dogs, birds ate birds. Even the gods ate each other. Why, he concluded therefore, should men not eat one another?

A Maori chief named Touai was brought to London in 1818 for civilizing. It did not go too well. He missed his feasts on human flesh, he told scandalized dinner parties. He was fed up with beef, he would then add, a faraway look in his eye. Women and children, now they were delicious. But never eat the flesh raw, he warned his enraptured companions. And they should always remember to keep the fat from the buttocks particularly, for dribbling on sweet potatoes.

The culinary details might be different, but the general meaning was widely shared. As nineteenth-century Congolese tribesmen explained it to one English missionary, the Reverend W. Holman

Bentley: 'You eat fowls and goats, and we eat men – why not?' When one chief of the Liboko tribe was asked about human flesh, he allegedly smacked his lips and expressed the desire to eat 'everyone on earth' (see Bentley, Bibliography).

Some Nigerian tribes had the same pragmatic approach. When curious anthropologists questioned members of the Mambila tribe, they were told in no uncertain terms that human flesh was just another form of meat. When an enemy was killed, he was usually eaten on the spot, without ritual or ceremony. The leftovers were taken home for the old, who loved them. The Azande of the southern Sudan had a similar attitude. They ate flesh because it was good meat, according to E.E. Evans-Pritchard, an early twentieth-century anthropologist. The Azande would say that strangers meant nothing to them. Nothing but meat, that is.

And meat is meat. The Mambila sold their dead to neighbouring tribes. Other tribes, in both Africa and South America, fattened up prisoners to take to market, often castrating them to speed up the process. Young boys were force-fed bananas, then baked and sold. In southern Nigeria there were going market prices for different cuts of the human victim; in the Congo lines of men and women – potential meals – were led around, their bodies marked up with coloured clay for purchasers to choose a cut. When an enraged European protested, the trader in question looked bemused. 'But that is not a man,' he said, 'it is a slave – beef' (see Askenasy, Bibliography).

It is all relative, of course. It was rarely just a matter of 'why not?'. Mambila males also believed that eating their enemies would transfer their courage, whilst Mambila females were prohibited from eating any human flesh. The pot an Azande used for cooking human flesh was only ever used by him, which suggests something special was going on. Even J.H.P. Murray's Papuans dressed their consumption of 'real food' in rituals. It was not considered acceptable to eat someone you had killed yourself, 'but if, after killing a man, you go and sit on a coconut, with also a coconut under each heel, and get your daughter to boil the man's heart, then you may drink the water in which the heart has been boiled. And you may eat a little of the heart also, but you must be sitting on the coconuts all the time' (see Hogg, Bibliography).

Cannibalism for its own sake undoubtedly existed. As long as humans were capable of dehumanizing the 'other', then the other could be seen as meat. It would be easier to think that people always found this difficult, and that that was why they usually needed to dress up their greed or culinary lust in ritual, religion or games with coconuts. Easy, but probably wrong. If a large number of highly-educated, twentieth-century Germans could bring themselves to believe that another group of talking bipeds were less than human, then it is hardly surprising that 'less developed' cultures – on every continent, of every race – have often had a hard job distinguishing one type of meat from another.

Modern-day Papuans can remember cannibalism in their lifetime; some tribes claim it is practised today by way of revenge

1: Cannibalism And Ritual

Feeding the gods, making magic

When Cortez and his invading army reached Mexico in the early sixteenth century, they found a culture built around industrial-scale human sacrifice and cannibalism. The Aztec creators of this culture had only been settled for a couple of centuries, and their remarkably elaborate religion had been cobbled together over the same period. Starting off with their own array of gods, they had borrowed more from other tribes, and filled any obvious gaps in their pantheon with new inventions. By the time Cortez arrived they had 'so many gods that even neighbouring peoples had never been able to put a number to them' (see Tannahill, Bibliography).

The Aztecs were keen – desperate, even – to keep the gods on their side. Trouble was expected. Humanity was already into a Fifth World, and the Aztecs were determined to save it from the fate of the previous four. No effort could be spared in their struggle to keep the sun in motion, and the monsters of the twilight at bay. The sun had been created by one god's sacrifice – he had thrown himself into a brazier – and set in motion by the blood and hearts of other gods. It seemed only fair, not to mention logical, that humans should provide their own sacrifices to keep the cosmos going. And since populations can get restive when their rulers start killing them in large numbers, most of the blood and hearts would have to come from foreigners. Therefore, a more-or-less permanent state of war, in which killing was frowned on and prisoner-taking prized, would have to waged. For the better part of two centuries, the armies of the Aztecs scoured Central America in search of foreign victims.

Festivals of food

The prisoners were brought back to Tenochtitlan in the central valley, there to await their moment of terror at one of the regular festivals. There were eighteen of these, one for each twenty-day month of the Aztec calendar, and only four were bloodless – three given over to flowers, and one to fasting.

The other fourteen were variations on the classic theme. The sacrificial victim was led to a temple altar – usually a slab of curved stone on the top of a step pyramid – and held down by five priests, one for each limb and one for the head. The head priest would then slice open the victim's

Equal shares: a human sacrifice, circa 1579. This ritual had very important religious and social meanings for the Aztecs

chest with an obsidian knife, cut out the still-beating heart, and hold it aloft to the sun. He would then place the heart in a bowl with burning incense, the smoke from the latter wafting the smell of blood heavenwards. The body was thrown – carried, if the victim had been noble or particularly brave – down the steps for use by the victim's captors.

The body was cut up and flayed. The head was hung on a skull rack, and one thigh was presented to the governing council. The leader of the captors was sometimes given the flayed skin – wearing it would bless him with the qualities of the victim. The rest of the flesh was divided between the local nobles and the other captors; the bones were given to the animals who guarded the temples.

Other sacrifices

Those sacrificed were not always men. At the year's first festival, dedicated to the rain god, children were drowned to avert drought. Their blood was kneaded into corn dough replicas of the war god Uitzilopochtli. The hearts of these replicas were eaten by the reigning monarch, the rest shared out among the nobles.

The second festival belonged to Xipe Tolec, the god of spring. Prisoners of war, the braver the better, were tied to frames

A temple sacrifice: eating cooked human meat from cooking jars before Mictlantecutli, the Aztec Lord of the Realm of the Dead

of timber above the soon-to-be-sown soil and used as targets by Aztec bowmen. Once their blood had enriched the land, those still living were sacrificed in the usual way. Their skin was worn by the priests of Xipe Tolec, dyed yellow to symbolize the new skin of vegetation that was soon to adorn the land.

The fifth festival was the year's greatest, held when the sun was at its highest in the sky. The principal victim was chosen a year earlier, and given twelve months of luxury living to remember. His final three weeks were spent with four beautiful 'brides'. On the day of the feast he suffered the usual fate, and then it all started again with the turn of his lucky successor.

And so on. More sacrifices to the rain, more sacrifices to the salt waters, to fire, to hunting and war. When the maize was nearly ripe a young woman was chosen, adorned in red and yellow robes and feathers and set to dance through the night. She was finally decapitated at dawn; the first ear of corn to be cut. Another woman lost her head to celebrate the harvest, thus signalling the start to another elaborate set of rituals. Her skin was flayed, and all but one thigh's worth was donned by a young man pretending to be the Earth Mother. He went to another temple, sacrificed four victims, and was then banished. The thigh piece was made into a mask and given to the maize god's high priest. He only wore it for a short time, however, before setting off for the skin's final designated resting place – the edge of the Aztec kingdom.

Power politics

Amidst all this blood and gore, the Aztecs' cannibalism seems almost incidental. It was an important part of their rituals, but not important in itself. There is no evidence that the Aztecs were particularly fond of eating human flesh, or that people were killed merely to provide meals. After the great siege of Tenochtitlan, in which many of the Aztec inhabitants starved to death, the Spanish noticed, somewhat reluctantly, that their enemy had not taken to cannibalizing their own dead.

If Mexico had boasted animals of a decent size, it is quite possible that the Aztecs would have 'progressed', as so many other cultures did, from human to animal sacrifice. But horses were extinct, cattle and sheep unknown, buffalo and caribou way beyond the northern horizon. No self-respecting culture could expect to keep the sun in motion by sacrificing mere turkeys.

There are those who claim that the Aztec religion provided what any religion has to provide – a reason for dying. Most of the victims believed, like their killers, that sacrifices were necessary to keep the cosmos in motion. They might have preferred to swap places, but at least they were doing their bit. There are others who claim that one blood-soaked tyranny is much like any other, and that the Aztec ruling class used their gods much the way other ruling classes used theirs, as the most cost-effective way of keeping their people terrified, and, in their case, supplied with fresh meat.

Hap! Hap! Hap!

During their conquest of the world between the fifteenth and nineteenth centuries, the Europeans came across many other cultures which made ceremonial use of cannibalism. The Kwakiutls, who lived in what is now southern British Columbia, were a classic case in point. Their cannibalism was just one element in a highly complex set of ritualized behaviours, all of which were designed to protect and benefit the tribe.

In his teens, each Kwakiutl male dedicated himself to one of the tribal gods. This served two purposes. The tribal god – rather like the Aztec sun – was thus encouraged to go on protecting the tribe, and the disciple, by following in his master's footsteps, was given the chance to acquire some of his attributes.

The most fearsome of these gods was Baxbakualauxsiwae (He-who-is-first-to-eat-man-at-the-mouth-of-the-river). The bear-like Baxbakualauxsiwae lived in the mountains, in a home forever belching blood-red smoke. He had a fearsome wife, and she had a fearsome slave; their joint vocation in life was supplying his many blood-stained mouths with human flesh. He also had specialist help – a slave raven named Qauxqoaxualanlxsiwae who pecked out eyes, another bird who could split skulls with his beak, and a large grizzly bear named Haialikilal who functioned as a minder.

Initiation as one of Baxbakualauxsiwae's disciples – or *Hamatsas* – was a long business. The initiate had to spend three months away from his village, learning to live like his sponsor. During that time he was required to visit his village once in the guise of Baxbakualauxsiwae, whistling and shouting 'Hap! Hap! Hap!' (which roughly translates as 'Eat! Eat! Eat!'), and trying to tear chunks out of people with his teeth. He was also required to smoke-cure a mummified corpse.

On the appointed day the existing *Hamatsas* arrived at the initiate's hut, and, in strict order of seniority, ate four pieces each. These were swallowed whole – chewing was strictly forbidden – and then forced back up again with saltwater emetics. Wading and dunking in water followed, and the whole ceremony climaxed in prolonged dancing. By the time it was over the new initiate had his licence to eat human flesh.

Using it was something else again. Though an *Hamatsa* could, theoretically at least, devour slaves or corpses at will, the disincentives were hard to ignore. After such a meal – which he was, in any case, required to throw up – the *Hamatsa* was

forbidden warm food or sex for sixteen days. The Kwakiutls did not eat their fellow men out of hunger.

The Leopard Men

The same could be said of Sierra Leone's Leopard Societies. They also used cannibalism as an integral part of their initiation ceremony, although in their case an innocent victim was sacrificed and the body actually consumed. The initiate was given an evening meal of human flesh, then sent into the forest with several companions for a night of non-stop roaring. Early the following morning the group ambushed their pre-arranged victim – usually an adolescent girl supplied by the initiate's family – and cut her throat with a ceremonial knife. The body was dissected, the innards examined for omens, and then cut into meal-size portions for a tribal feast. Skin from the forehead and fat from the kidneys were used in creating a ceremonial effigy, which was given to the victim's mother and father.

This ritual was supposed to make 'medicine' or magic, to shed one person's blood for the overall good of the tribe. It is more than probable that society members actually believed this, but just as likely that they enjoyed the ceremony too. Wrapping up self-interest in complicated belief systems is one of the oldest of human habits.

Ritual

Another murderous ritual hails from the South American country of Guyana. The perpetrators were – some say still are – tribal sorcerers known as Kainamàs. Their

A Kwakiutl mask representing Tsonoqa, a giantess who carried children away to eat them. She announced her presence by whistling

Culture clash: from the Malay Archipelago, two Dyak headhunters (a Saghai on the right and a Loondoo in the middle). On the far right, a priest

first attacks on their chosen victim – any hapless soul who happens to be on the wrong forest path at the wrong time – are meant to disable. A dislocated neck, a hand of broken fingers – anything to slow the victim down, and leave him or her in lasting pain. The second attack, which takes place months or even years later, involves the introduction of toxins and sharp objects into both mouth and anus. A few days after death, the Kainamà pushes a stick into the decomposing corpse, pulls it out and sucks it. This act of low-level cannibalism is apparently an essential part of the whole process, as it is seen to secure heavenly protection for the Kainamà from the wrath of the victim's relatives.

Head hunters

The Dyaks of Borneo are famous for being headhunters, but they did not hunt for trophies. Throughout what is now Indonesia, the head was considered the seat of a person's essential being, of his or her 'soul substance'. This substance, so essential to life, could be poured on the fields, so fertilising the grain and keeping the tribe alive. As the early twentieth-century British anthropologist E.O. James noted, 'Headhunting is largely prompted by the idea of securing additional soul-substance to increase the productivity of the soil and, indirectly, the fertility of the tribesmen and tribeswomen. It adds to the vital essence in the village: hence it is essential that as many heads as possible shall be acquired. Just as the Aztecs carried on wars to secure sacrificial victims, so the head-hunting expeditions become a normal feature of native life' (see James, Bibliography).

Mau Mau initiation

More recently, the initiation rites introduced by the Mau Mau rebels in 1950s Kenya contained significant elements of cannibalism. There were eight different oaths for the eight different ranks in the Mau Mau army, and the ceremonies that accompanied each promotion all featured some sort of human food. The raw recruit was started gently on a mixture of sheep's blood and his own; by the time he made general he was eating a medley of white man, made from pulverized wrist bones, blood and excrement. Field marshals were fed the brains and heart of, respectively, a man and a child murdered for the purpose. This was all done for 'the magic by which they hoped to bring white supremacy to an end' (see Tannahill, Bibliography).

Eating the enemy

'At about twelve o'clock a long procession of men marched through the [missionary] station laden with spoil. Fifty men carried as many goats, most of which had been speared; others, less fortunate, brought away fish-nets, stools and plantain. Whilst this was proceeding, as a kind of introduction to what would follow, two men passed, one carrying a human neck poised aloft upon a spear, the other an arm; both had been lopped off an unfortunate man who had been killed and left on the field. Later on, we were horrified by a more ghastly sight. A party of warriors returned who had joined somewhat late in the chase. They marched in single file past our house. In the middle of the line three men bore the remaining parts of the mutilated body. One carried the still bleeding trunk; he had slung the other arm through a large wound in the abdomen and, suspended on this, the ghastly burden swung at his side. Two others shouldered the legs...we were assured that these would be cooked and eaten in the evening' (see Bentley, Bibliography).

The enemy had been vanquished, and, as has been the habit at one time or another in all parts of the world, was about to be consumed. This particular scene was witnessed by a missionary named Walter Stapleton, who had set up a Baptist mission in the 1890s among the dreaded Bangala tribes of the Congo basin. He admitted to bad dreams for several nights thereafter.

The Bangalas, as far as is known, ate the enemy for no other reason than that he was the enemy. The Amazonian Majeronas and Nigerian Kaleri operated on much the same basis; anyone who ventured into their territory was fair game for killing and eating. The Amazonian Mangeromas set traps in the jungle, and the late nineteenth-century explorer Algot Lange was on hand to witness a patrol returning with the bodies of two Peruvian *mestizos*. Once the hands and feet had been removed, the corpses were taken to the chief, who 'nodded his head and smiled'. A communal feast was prepared, leaving Lange wondering how long it would be 'before they would forget themselves and place my own extremities in those same pots and pans?' (see Lange, Bibliography).

The African meat trade

Many tribes ate those killed in the regular conflicts between them. Some used the bodies of the slain to supplement their normal diet, while others had more of an eye for a profit, selling prisoners they could not eat at one of the many cannibal markets. Some hardly bothered with the eating, and concentrated on the profits, mounting raids into the jungle for sellable human meat. One missionary, the Reverend W. Holman Bentley, writing in the late nineteenth century, described the trade: 'They would paddle down the Lulongo, cross the main river when the wind was not blowing, make up [capture]

Communal cannibalism was obviously a popular event in parts of South America, as this image from 1602 shows

A grizzly looking barbeque of human remains in the New Hebrides (west of Fiji). The picture was taken as late as the 1920s

...two missionaries came across...a human trunk lying in the surf, a head sitting in a nearby canoe [and] pairs of arms and legs roasting on an open fire...

the Mobangi and sell their freight in some of the towns for ivory. The purchasers would then feed up their starvelings until they were fat enough for the market, then butcher them and sell the meat in small joints' (see Bentley, Bibliography).

For such tribes, human meat was pure product. Others were more interested in the culinary experience, and devised their arrangements accordingly. The Amazonian Cobeus used to make war for the sole purpose of eating their enemies. In New Caledonia the women would follow their men to the battlefield, dig their ovens at the rear, and, assuming the men proved victorious, comb the ground for the best-looking corpses. The returning warriors liked their food fresh.

Revenge beyond killing

Of course enemies are not always found on a battlefield. Killing and eating has a long political pedigree, particularly among impulsive autocrats. The ancient Chinese ruler Chou Wang was so angered by the criticism of several high officials that he had them killed and served up. Confucius, who seems such a pragmatist in most Western tomes, told those whose parents had been killed that their revenge should go way beyond killing – the enemy should be

consumed *in toto*, even down to the bones.

Cannibalising someone has always been seen as a wonderful way of expressing utter scorn, too. The member of the Palestinian resistance group Black September who assassinated the Jordanian politician Wasfi Tal (the man responsible for enforcing the expulsion of the Palestinians in 1970–1) only expressed himself satisfied after he had drunk his victim's blood.

Revenge ranks high among the motives cited for duty cannibalism. After a massacre in the New Hebrides two missionaries came across a rather horrifying beach tableau: a human trunk lying in the surf, a head sitting in a nearby canoe, pairs of arms and legs roasting on an open fire. The victim, it transpired, had been a chief and, as the missionaries soon found out, he had had it coming to him – a few weeks earlier he had been responsible for luring two men onto his own island for murder and consumption.

Easter Island seems to have had an almost Sicilianesque culture, in which single acts of cannibalism – sometimes carried out for the best of cultural reasons – spawned long chains of tit-for-tat reprisals. After eating someone in revenge, the eaters were fond of opening their mouths to the victims' relatives and remarking that 'your flesh has stuck between my teeth' (see Metraux, Bibliography). Hardly surprisingly, this rarely ended the matter.

In New Guinea there was even a word, *maiha*, for someone eaten in revenge for a previous meal. The capture, display and consumption of one *maiha* feature in a story from early twentieth-century anthropologist C.G. Seligmann's academic treatise on the island's Melanesian inhabitants. Members of the Maivara tribe intercepted a canoe from Wagawaga, and took its crew – a man and a girl – prisoner. They then headed for home via Wagawaga, stopping offshore to gloat over their naked captives and shout out details of their imminent consumption. The man was eaten forthwith and the girl was adopted by a Maivara woman.

The enraged Wagawaga set out to find a *maiha*. Entering Maivara territory by night, they surrounded an isolated hut and took its unlucky inhabitant prisoner. Now it was their turn to loiter offshore and hurl insults at their raging enemy. Once back on home territory they took their time killing the prisoner, spearing, wounding and blinding him before roasting him in a fire of dry coconut leaves.

The *Boyd* massacre

Europeans were seldom witnesses to such appalling sport, but those passengers who boarded the brigantine *Boyd* for its voyage from Australia to England in 1810 were given a front seat to their own demise. One of the passengers was TeAara, the son of Maori chieftain Piopio. He was supposedly working his passage home to New Zealand, and when he refused to do anything Captain Thompson had him flogged. This proved something of an own goal; the moment the ship arrived at the boy's home port of Whangaroa, TeAara scuttled off to tell his father all about his humiliation. Revenge was called for.

Three days later Captain Thompson and four other men headed upriver in their longboat. They were looking for suitable trees to fell, and imagined that the Maori canoes behind them were providing an escort. But the moment the Europeans landed they were attacked, killed, stripped and carted back to the Maori village for a feast. The killers waited till dusk, then put on their victims' clothes and headed back towards the *Boyd* in the longboat. Most of the other Europeans were taken by surprise, killed and dismembered on deck, while a few fortunate escapees watched from high in the rigging. These were caught later, when another Maori chief tried to intervene on their behalf.

There was no happy ending for Piopio and TeAara. After towing the *Boyd* upriver they searched the hold for weapons and

> **When the European rescue mission finally arrived...the only remains were teeth-marked bones scattered around the burnt-out boat.**

Baptême d'un Captif.
Bautismo de un Cautivo   Battesimo d'un prigioniero.

Unsurprisingly, Europeans did their best to stop such 'heathen' practices as cannibalism. In Brazil, missionaries were allowed to baptise those on their way to the pot, but only with a cloth and not by immersion, so as not to spoil the meat

carried the muskets and gunpowder they found up onto the deck. As one man forced open one of the gunpowder barrels, Piopio playfully struck a flint, blowing himself, his son and half his warriors to smithereens. When the European rescue mission finally arrived, there was hardly anyone left to either rescue or punish.

Only four of the seventeen Europeans – a woman, a teenage boy, a young child and a baby – were still living. The only remains of the rest were teeth-marked bones scattered around the burnt-out boat.

Punishment and deterrence

Cannibalism has often served as a suitably

dramatic way of punishing an opponent or enemy. The Nigerian Sura tribe, for example, ate criminals and adulterers. One Congolese chief told his local missionary, the aforementioned Reverend Bentley, that he had recently killed and eaten one of his seven wives. The woman had broken both tribal and family law, and he had decided to make an example of her. His other six wives had much enjoyed the feast.

In China, a provincial governor found guilty of disloyalty to the Emperor was likely to be killed and decapitated. In some cases his head was then served up to the other governors as a loyalty bonus. In one variation on this theme, the Sui Emperor Yang Ti (circa AD 600) had an official named Hu Hsi-cheng arrested for disloyalty, butchered and broiled, and fed to his fellow officials. Those who really tucked in were commended and showered with gifts.

Chinese generals who failed their political masters occasionally ended up as a meal, and outright traitors risked worse. Nan-kung Wan and Meng Huo, who killed their Sung lord in 685 BC, were chopped, pickled and kept in a jar. In some places and times, executed Chinese prisoners were cannibalized, either by the executioner or by those to whom he sold the rights.

Sometimes the point was just to scare the opposition. The sixteenth-century French explorer, Jean de Lery, put some thought to the motives of the Tupinamba, a cannibalistic tribe in what is now south-east Brazil. After noting that culinary taste and hunger for revenge both played a significant role, he came to the conclusion that the Tupinambas' chief intention was that 'by pursuing the dead and gnawing them right down to the bone, they will strike fear and terror into the hearts of the living' (see Korn, Radice and Hawes, Bibliography). The Chinese Emperor presumably had much the same effect in mind when he invited his provincial governors to feast on their associate's head.

Unbridled savagery

And then there was the sadism. The Bafum-Bansaw of West Africa tortured their prisoners by forcing boiling palm oil into their stomachs and bowels. The supposed reason for the dual enema was to make the flesh more succulent; the hideous pain was just a bonus.

In the Marquesas Islands, prisoners fared even worse. According to A.P. Rice (see Rice, Bibliography): 'They broke their [captives'] legs to prevent them from attempting to escape before being eaten, but kept them alive so that they could brood over their impending fate. Their arms were broken so that they could not retaliate in any way against their maltreatment. The Marquesans threw them on the ground and leaped on their chests so that their ribs were broken and

> **Australian aboriginals drank the blood of their elders to absorb their strength, and to make themselves part of the tribe's ancestoral life**

pierced their lungs, so that they could not even voice protests…Rough poles were thrust up through the natural orifices of their bodies and slowly turned in their intestines. Finally, when the hour had come for them to be prepared for the feast, they were spitted on long poles that entered between their legs and emerged from their mouths…' It is difficult to see how such treatment acted as a deterrent, since all the tribes in the islands were handing out this sort of punishment.

Transference

Whatever the prime motivation for eating an enemy – be it revenge, anger, hunger or political advantage – a secondary reason was often present. By taking the flesh of another body into one's own, the consumer could imagine he or she was imbibing the qualities which that body had only recently possessed – its power, wisdom, sexual potency, youthfulness. The Aztecs were far from alone in believing that their victims' life-force was transferable by consumption. Indeed, it has seemed a commonsensical notion to most of the people ever born on this planet.

Ancient Egyptian soldiers believed it. Scythian horsemen and African villagers believed it. The Chinese seemed

particularly smitten with the idea. Eunuch officials in Ming China sought to recover their genitals by feasting on the brains of young male virgins – hardly enemies in the usual sense, but typecast for the purpose. There is no record of it working. Human blood and flesh were commonly held to promote sexual potency, and as recently as the 1890s soldiers in Taiwan were caught consuming the latter for that very purpose. In both the nineteenth century Taiping Rebellion and twentieth century civil war there were stories of human hearts being consumed by soldiers in pursuit of strength, sexual stamina or both.

Many African tribes believed in transference, and arranged their menus accordingly. The Mambilas, Sura and Kukukuku all saved the best cuts for their growing boys and young warriors, hoping to tap the strength of their dead foes. The Ganawuri, Rubakuba and Zumperi took the opposite course, handing them on to the old for purposes of rejuvenation.

Australian aborigines drank the blood of their elders to absorb their strength, and to make themselves part of the tribe's ancestral life. When it came to enemies, they were more literal-minded – eating his heart transferred his strength and eating his brain took in his knowledge.

Cannibalism as renewal

The eating of dead enemies, while often understandable, was usually done for selfish motives. The deceased was not expected to benefit from his own consumption. The eating of friends and relatives, on the other hand, usually had a selfless component. The consumers might benefit from the resulting transference – as the virtues of the deceased were passed on through his or her remains – but the dead also received some cosmic compensation. As one tribesman was recorded as saying, it was better to be inside a warm friend than buried in the cold earth.

The practice of mortuary cannibalism seems to have been most common in lowland South America, though that might simply reflect the huge number of twentieth-century anthropologists who visited the region. Amazonia, after all, was one of the last areas on earth to have 'undiscovered' tribes and uncorrupted cultures. In the 1970s, an anthropologist visiting the Guiaca in their Upper Orinoco homeland could still watch local tribespeople collect bones from the crematorial fire, grind them down with a wooden mortar, and mix them with plantain soup for the ceremonial lamentations.

There were variations on the theme. Some tribes roasted the flesh of their dead, but most restricted themselves to the bones. The Cashibos, Cobeus, Tarianos and Tucanos all pulverized the bones and mixed them in fermented drinks like *caxiri* (a beer made from manioc). The latter two tribes disinterred the decomposed corpses a month after the funeral, and left them in a huge pan over a fire until they were reduced to a black, carbonaceous mass. This was then ground into a fine powder for mixing with *caxiri*, and drunk by everyone present.

The Wari

The Wari lived – and continue to live – in western Brazil, deep in what is left of the Amazon jungle. They were not discovered until the 1950s, when they were still practising different types of cannibalism. Enemy intruders – they recognized no other kind – were killed and eaten for the reasons outlined in the previous chapter. Their corpses were treated in ways that expressed hostility and hatred. But the Waris also ate the flesh, organs and bones of their own dead. These were treated with love and respect.

Why did they eat their own dead? Not because they liked the taste, and not because they needed meat. Consuming the dead was a show of compassion and

As one tribesman explained to a European visitor, it was better to be inside a warm friend than buried in the cold earth.

The Wari are a very close-knit culture. Familial ties are very important and social duties to relations extend well into death

respect for the dead person's relatives. A corpse-in-being, whether buried or not, offered a constant reminder of loss, a focus for all the memories that prolonged the period of grieving. Eating the corpse was eating the grief. They also did it to 'please the dead person's spirit' (see Conklin, Bibliography). Staying 'within' the tribe was much more amenable than being left to rot in the ground.

People were not allowed to eat their own close relatives. They ate human flesh as a service for other families, and other families did it for them. A service, moreover, which was often none too pleasant – the decayed state of many corpses hardly made for a convivial meal. Performing this service was a recognition of an individual's social obligations, the practice itself a force for social cohesion.

The practice does make human sense. While our culture deals with its dead the same way it deals with its rubbish – through burning or burial – the Wari did with their dead what we do with things we like – they put them in their mouths.

But not any more. The Catholic priests, Protestant evangelists and government bureaucrats who swarmed all over the newly-discovered tribe were appalled by the Waris' cannibalistic habits, and made their abolition a top priority. The newly decimated Waris – 60 per cent of the tribe were soon killed off by diseases for which they had no

immunity – were horrified at this attack on their customs, but powerless to object. 'I do not know if you can understand this,' one Wari told anthropologist Beth Conklin, 'because you have never had a child die... but it is a sad thing to put his body in the earth...it is cold in the earth...we keep remembering our child lying there, cold. We remember, and we are sad' (see Conklin, Bibliography).

The indignity of decay

Such customs were widespread. Askenasy lists the Scythians, Tibetans and several Australian tribes among those who consumed their dead out of pity. A.P. Elkin, in his history of the Australian aborigines, describes a burial ceremony in Queensland in which the body, its organs removed, is dried in the sun. The flesh is eaten, the rest – the dry bones and skin – is packed into a bundle for either burial, cremation or placing in a hollow tree. 'Cannibalism was considered a most honourable rite,' Elkin says, 'to be used only for persons of worth' (see Elkin, Bibliography). As with the Wari, eating the dead was a mark of respect and affection.

The extent of such practices in Africa is hard to judge, but eating the dead as an act of reverence was not uncommon. Some east African tribes would keep the dried flesh of their dead relatives in readiness for special guests, who refused it at their peril. The Bagesu

> **A dead relative forced to suffer the indignity of decay would have every justification for anger, and would doubtless return to haunt the living.**

tribe of Uganda had a ritual for eating their own dead which differed from the South American example in several ways. The Bagesu insisted, in particular, on apparent secrecy. Everyone in the village knew what was going on, but it was part of the rigual that they had to pretend that they did not.

The Royal Society's John Roscoe

The Wari are from a sophisiticated culture, as this pottery figure in a jaguar costume, from AD 600–700, shows

observed the process at work. When a man died, his relatives were summoned to his house for the period of mourning, which began, if possible, on the evening of his death. As it began to grow dark, the body was taken to a piece of waste ground nearby, and apparently left for the jackals. The male relatives cemented this illusion by hiding nearby and making jackal noises. This would serve the purpose of tipping off the other villagers, who made sure they kept themselves and their children indoors. Once night had fallen the senior female relatives went out to the body, cut it up, and carried what they needed back to the house, leaving the rest to be consumed by the local wildlife. 'For the next three, or sometimes four, days,' Roscoe wrote, 'the relatives mourned in the house in which the death had taken place, and there they cooked and ate the flesh of the dead, destroying the bones by fire and leaving nothing' (see Roscoe, Bibliography).

Why did they say they did this? A dead relative forced to suffer the indignity of decay would have every justification for anger, and would doubtless return to haunt the living. Eating him preserved his dignity, averted the haunting and provided his relations with food.

A helping hand

Making positive use of the dead by eating them does not seem like such an outlandish idea. Making positive use of the living by offering up their flesh for food seems a lot stranger, but has, in the past, proved almost as common. The Chinese, in particular, have a long tradition of expressing loyalty and devotion by feeding their slaves, their relations or themselves to someone else.

In the seventh century BC there was the famous case of I Ya, whose master was always hungering after new culinary experiences. I Ya killed his own son, steamed him, and served him up on a plate. Another old legend concerns a family caught in a siege. A man was about to be eaten when his wife, fearing that the family line would end with him, offered herself in his place. A different sort of sacrifice crops up in several legends, such as the general who gallantly drank a soup made out of his son, rather than betray his country. An unusual situation perhaps, but poignant nevertheless.

The human body as a medicine cabinet

The Chinese usually fed themselves to each other for medicinal reasons. One ancient legend featured an emperor who banished his daughter for refusing to marry, then sent her a message saying how near he was to death, and how much in need of her hands and eyes. She did the necessary gouging and cutting, and posted off the body parts. He had them ground up, swallowed them, and was cured. Her compensation was promotion to goddess – Guan Yin, 'she of the thousand eyes and arms'.

Less legendary donors also go back a long way. During the Tang dynasty a young woman from Chekiang named Li Miao-ning allegedly saved her sick in-laws by cutting three pieces of flesh from her thigh and making them into a restorative soup. She was far from alone – the Imperial records for this period list twenty-four recorded cases of *ko ku* or cannibalism-for-the-family, most involving thighs and upper arms, a few involving livers and breasts. Tang physicians were obviously impressed; it was around this time that human flesh first featured as a curative in medical textbooks.

Others were less keen. In 1261 extracting one's own liver was officially banned, and nine years later thighs joined the forbidden list. But people kept cutting, believing more in the efficacy of tradition than authority. Li Sheng-shan died after cutting out his liver for his sick mother; her fate is not recorded. Chang San-ai sliced out part of his liver with one hand and staunched the bleeding with the other; both he and his mother allegedly survived. Other stories had a sadder ending. When Chu Cheng-yu got sick, his wife Ts'ao cut flesh from her arms in an attempt (which proved fatal) to save him. Her parents took legal action against the husband and his parents, claiming that they forced Ts'ao into the sacrifice. Another series of imperial edicts in 1652 banned the medical consumption of a woman's flesh by her husband.

A slightly fanciful image? Dated circa 1885, the inhabitants of China Town, San Francisco, are shown consuming their dead

A case of *ko ku* was reported as recently as 1987, but the woman concerned was – unlike her similarly inclined ancestors – pronounced mentally unstable. A similar anathema now attaches to the once-common use of body parts harvested from the dead. In his sixteenth-century classic *Pen Ts'ao Kang Mu*, Li Shih-chen identified medicinal uses for thirty-five human body parts, but these days such cannibalism is mostly frowned upon. There are still believers, however – in 1995 a flourishing illegal market in human foetuses was uncovered in Hong Kong.

2: Cultural Cannibalism

Menus

The traditional cannibal recipe, as any *aficionado* of black and white movies will know, can be stated in a couple of sentences. 'Take one whole missionary and place in giant pot. Boil until ready.' Like most Hollywood versions of reality, this is more than a little simplistic. The human race has devoted just as much ingenuity to the preparation and cooking of its own flesh as it has to any other form of meat.

Which humans, and which of their parts, were considered the tastiest? That depended on where and who you happened to be. Most cannibal tribes seem to have preferred women to men, and young to old, but there were exceptions. The Liberian Bele found women bitter, and the Maoris were keen on black men of around fifty. The preference for black over white seems to have been almost universal, perhaps on account of the latter's saltier diet.

When it comes to parts, it is hard to find one that was not considered a delicacy by

Barbeque Brazilian style, from a French engraving dated 1528-98

The Liberian Bele found women bitter, and the Maoris were keen on black men of around fifty.

some tribe or other. In Fiji a woman's thigh and upper arm were preferred, while the African Tangale specialized in women's heads. More predictably perhaps, female breasts were on many male menus, and genitals in general had a wide popularity. Penises roasted in hot ash were a particular favourite. Some Nigerian tribes rated the palms, fingers and toes, while the Ibos had a curious passion for knuckles. Hearts and brains were fairly universal choices, but eyes, cheeks and unborn children were more singular tastes.

Preparation

There were many varied and imaginative methods of preparation. Mention has already been made of the Bafum-Bansaw method of enema-marination. Several tribes steeped their prospective meal in water for several days, thus tenderizing the meat and allowing easier removal of the skin. The African Bassange checked the efficacy of the process by cutting off the head and offering it to the local ants. If they ate, all was well. Some tribes poured boiling water over prisoners to flay them – alive, of course – in preparation for killing and cooking them. Others preferred to bury the bodies for a while and then disinter them; most were dissected in one way or another, either

delimbed, disembowelled or cut up completely.

The cooking took many forms. Some humans were boiled in pots, but rarely whole. Baking was widely popular, often in hole-ovens lined with heated stones. Roasting was an almost universal practice, though methods varied. The Kjarawas of Nigeria, for example, wrapped bodies in mud before placing them in the fire, which had the added benefit of removing all the hair. Sun-broiling was used to cook the living and the dead, particularly in the Pacific. Smoke-drying and pickling were the most common methods of preservation.

The Chinese had a particular preference for steaming, and their human mince dumplings were sufficiently popular in Yuan and Ming times to warrant frequent mentions in the well known *Water Margin* stories. They were also adept at pickling their prisoners of war, using two main methods – *hai* (chopping and pickling in wine) and *t'so* (mincing and pickling in salt). The Chinese have always varied their methods of cooking more than other cultures, and those eleventh century Chinese restaurants which served human meat are said to have offered a highly comprehensive menu – people of all ages prepared in a dazzling variety of styles.

The cannibal isles

Fiji comprises over three hundred islands spread across half a million square miles of the south-western Pacific. When the Europeans first interested themselves in Fijian affairs during the middle third of the nineteenth century, these islands were divided into many small territories, each ruled by its own chief. These territories were banded together in ever-shifting confederacies, and the confederacies, rather in the manner of Orwell's *1984*, were almost constantly at war with each other. These endless wars were not fought for territory, loot or slaves, but for oven-fodder. It was not for nothing that Fiji was nicknamed 'the Cannibal Isles'.

Missionaries

There is a wealth of evidence concerning cannibalism in Fiji. The missionaries came, saw and promptly wrote home demanding money. The more lurid the picture they painted, the more money they were likely to get, and they wrote accordingly.

'… BAKED HUMAN BEINGS – not one, nor two, nor ten, but twenty, thirty, forty, fifty at a single feast!' as one missionary almost gleefully reported. 'We have heard on credible authority of 200 human beings having been thus devoured on one of these occasions. The writer of this APPEAL has himself conversed with persons who have seen forty and fifty eaten at a single sitting – eaten without anything like disgust; eaten indeed with a high relish!' (see Hogg, Bibliography).

The missionaries realized that cannibalism was an integral part of Fijian life, but seemed either reluctant or incapable of asking themselves why this should be. They took note of the Fijians' down-to-earth acceptance of the practice, recorded the cruelties involved in the hunting, gathering and cooking of the food, and put the whole business down to simple evil. Words like 'diabolical', 'revolting' and 'fiendish' figured prominently in their letters home. Their obvious self-interest in exaggerating Fijian cannibalism encouraged some later anthropologists to make the opposite mistake, and deny its importance to Fijian culture. Fortunately, the wealth of oral-historical and archaeological evidence which gradually became available over the next century proved that cannibalism was indeed crucial to the way Fijian culture worked. This evidence also provided confirmation that the missionaries' observations, though exaggerated, misinterpreted and coloured by moral outrage, were essentially accurate.

A question of culture

It was perhaps easy to mistake the Fijian acceptance of cannibalism for callousness. There was a definite 'Why not?' aspect to the Fijian attitude, who did not agree that there was anything questionable in their culinary culture. 'The Feegeeans eat human flesh not merely from a principle of revenge, nor from necessity, but from choice', the Reverend Cargill wrote. Observing a new delivery, he noted that 'the children amused themselves by sporting with and mutilating

> **The missionaries realized that cannibalism was an integral part of Fijian life, but seemed either reluctant or incapable of asking themselves why this should be.**

the body of a little girl. A crowd of men and women maltreated the body of a grey-haired old man and that of a young woman. Human entrails were floating down the river...' (see Hogg, Bibliography).

Fifty years later, Alfred St. Johnston reported that Fijians 'loved human flesh for its own sake', and that a man 'would order to be clubbed some man or woman that he considered would be good for cooking, his plea being that his "back tooth was aching" and only human flesh could cure it' (see St. Johnston, Bibliography). St. Johnston believed that this matter-of-fact attitude towards cannibalism was at least partly explained by the unavailability of other meat – the next largest animal available to nineteenth-century Fijians was the rat. And for

anthropologist A.P. Rice this was reason enough – Fijian cannibalism was simply 'a most natural appetite for good red meat' (see Rice, Bibliography).

Unnecessary cruelty

The missionaries were also struck by the levels of cruelty on display. 'When [the victim is] about to be immolated,' Cargill wrote, 'he is made to sit on the ground with his feet under his thighs and his hands placed before him. He is then bound so that he cannot move a limb or joint. In this posture he is placed on stones heated for the occasion (and some of them are red-hot), and then covered with leaves and earth, to be roasted alive' (see Hogg, Bibliography).

Another missionary named Jaggar told of prisoners being forced to dig their own ovens and collect firewood for their own immolation. 'Seru, the Bau chief, then had their arms and legs cut off, cooked and eaten, some of the flesh being presented to them. He then ordered a fish-hook to be put into their tongues, which were then drawn out as far as possible before being cut off. They were roasted and eaten, to the taunts of: "We are eating your tongues!"' (see Hogg, Bibliography).

Cruelty indeed, and to what end? None

The launching of a new canoe, for example, would require at least one human sacrifice and, as for the Aztecs, consumption was just part of the process. For Fijians, it was the most important part; cannibalism was a crucial component of the way the whole culture operated.

that the missionaries could see. To them, it seemed cruelty for cruelty's sake, more damning evidence of Fijian depravity, a wealth of lost souls to bring home to the Lord. That the Fijians had gods of their own was vaguely appreciated, but hardly taken seriously – what could such savages know of true religion?

And even more so, what respect could they therefore be expected to have for the religions of others? In 1874, an officer aboard HMS *Challenger*, one H. N. Moseley, recorded in his diary that some cannibals had been caught 'dragging the naked body of a missionary's wife through the jungle in order to eat it'.

The way the gods saw it

To continue Cargill's story of the live roasting – 'When cooked he is taken out of the oven and, his face and other parts painted black, that he may resemble a living man ornamented for a feast or for war, he is carried to the temple of gods and, being still retained in a sitting posture, is offered as a propitiatory sacrifice' (see Hogg, Bibliography).

The heads, it seems, were always turned over to the priests for religious ceremonies, which were many and various. The launching of a new canoe, for example, would require at least one human sacrifice

and, as for the Aztecs, consumption was part of the process. For Fijians, it was the most important part; cannibalism was a critical component of the way the whole culture operated.

When Fijians went to war, there was little credit in killing enemies – it was remembering to bring them home that counted. As a passing British sailor noted: 'Much more is thought of the savage who kills one man and carries him home than of the individual who may kill a hundred and let their dead bodies fall into the hands of the enemy' (see Endicott, Bibliography). Bringing the corpses home was a ceremony in itself. With limbs tied, the painted bodies were threaded together on poles, carried back to the village and thrown at the feet of the chief and priests. The heads would be cracked open on the braining stone outside the temple, thus offering intellectual sustenance to the gods. The bodies would be taken for cooking and eating, the choice parts going to the chief and priests, whose privileged connection with the gods allowed them to pass on enemy souls for destruction. The rest was divided up among the people, who thus shared both the meat and message.

One of the cannibals mentioned in Moseley's records, caught dragging a missionary's murdered wife home to eat

The evolution of cannibalism

The word 'cannibal' made its first appearance on 11 December 1492. Christopher Columbus had picked up the word from the peace-loving Arawaks, who used the word *caniba* – usually snarled – to describe their war-like neighbours the Cariba or Caribs. 'The Caniba', Columbus wrote in his journal, 'are none other than the people of the Great Khan, who must be neighbours to these. They have ships, they come and capture these people, and as those who are taken never return, the others believe that they have been eaten' (see Korn, Radice and Hawes, Bibliography).

Columbus was wrong about the Great Khan – Mongolia was and is some distance from the Caribbean – but was he wrong about the Caribs? On his second voyage he enjoyed a close encounter on the island of Guadeloupe. One of his shore parties came back with several women, who insisted that their Carib captors were indeed cannibals. Columbus himself saw human skulls and a basket of bones in one abandoned village, and it seemed highly likely that they were cannibals.

Confirmatory evidence piled up. Encountering four memberless natives, the Spanish decided they had been castrated to fatten them up. There were tales of other victims split in two, the limbs eaten, the rest salted. The fact that salting was unknown in the Caribbean until the Europeans arrived was inconvenient, but soon forgotten. Europeans were soon arguing over which meat the Caribs preferred – English, French, Spanish or Dutch. The Caribs, meanwhile, were dying in their multitudes from diseases unwittingly imported by the Europeans.

Mexican food

Thirty years on, Cortez and his colleagues invaded Mexico. The conquistadors were expecting the worst, their noses twitching in anticipation of blood's pagan smell from the moment they landed. They were not disappointed. The road inland to Tenochtitlan was littered with blood-strewn temples, and full of locals willing to speak about their eating habits. Like Columbus, Cortez seem to have had no trouble understanding the local dialect, and was sure enough of being understood to offer a series of sermons on the right way to live; human sacrifice, robbery and sodomy were to be abandoned forthwith. Cannibalism was never far from the conquistadors' minds – 'How anxious these traitors are to see us among the ravines so that they can gorge themselves on our flesh', wrote Cortez, after one ambush, adding

The Caribs and Aztecs were enthusiastic cannibals. This was highly convenient for the European invaders, who both wanted and needed to paint the natives as savages.

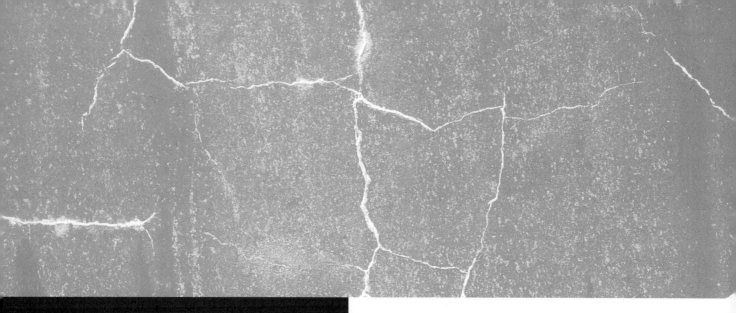

The road inland to Tenochtitlan was littered with blood-strewn temples, and full of locals willing to speak about their eating habits.

that salt, pepper and tomatoes were already waiting for them in the pot (see Tannahill, Bibliography).

The Caribs and Aztecs were enthusiastic cannibals. This was highly convenient for the European invaders, who both wanted and needed to paint the natives as savages. This was partly ideological – the apparent moral superiority of white Christian culture could be used to justify forced conversions, land theft, colonization and, eventually, genocide. It was also purely practical – in 1503, Queen Isabella of Spain introduced a decree stating that only cannibal Native Americans could be legally enslaved. Seven years later, Pope Innocent III provided a religious sugar-coating for this enslavement of the continent. Cannibalism, he declared, was a sin deserving to be punished by Christians through force of arms. Hardly surprisingly, eye-witness accounts of cannibalistic depravity started coming in from all over the Americas. Just as predictably, no effort was made to understand how cannibalism fitted into Native American culture, or how it functioned as one component of a politico-religious system which gave shape and sense to life. Carib and Aztec cannibalism was simply denounced as proof of their savagery.

Eating Christ

Christians, the implicit message went, could not possibly countenance such a practice. However, what of the Eucharist? Christianity had been born in an act of sacrifice which the Aztecs would have instantly understood. Christian worship, moreover, still centred around this one ritual – the Eucharist – which was seemingly totally cannibalistic.

Jesus Christ had sacrificed himself for humanity, a point he underlined at the Last Supper: 'Take, eat; this is my body which is given for you,' he said of the bread. 'This is my blood of the new testament, which is shed for you,' he said of the wine. According to Paul, Jesus accompanied his bread-breaking and wine-passing with the phrase, 'Do this in

In the Mass ceremony, bread and wine – or substitutes thereof – are consumed by worshippers in remembrance and reconfirmation of their faith.

The body and blood of Christ: missionaries struggled to stop the 'heathens' eating one another when it emerged the missionaries themselves regularly ate the body of their god

remembrance of me', and Christians have followed his injunction ever since. In the Mass ceremony bread and wine – or substitutes thereof – are consumed by worshippers in remembrance and reconfirmation of their faith.

But were the consecrated bread and wine merely symbolic substitutes for Christ's flesh and blood? Or did the ritual involve a genuine transubstantiation, a turning of the bread and wine into Christ's real flesh and blood? Opinions were divided from the outset. One Archbishop of Constantinople insisted that Christ 'gave us his body pierced with nails, that we might hold it in our hands and eat it, as a proof of his love' (see Jacob, Bibliograpy), but the majority of opinion was less ready for such a literal interpretation. This situation lasted until 1215, when Pope Innocent III unilaterally decided for transubstantiation. There was nothing symbolic about it, he said: the bread and wine were the flesh and blood of Christ. And that has been Rome's judgement ever since.

The early spread of this doctrine had one

> **...[does] the ritual involve a genuine transubstantiation, a turning of the bread and wine into Christ's real flesh and blood? Opinions were divided from the outset.**

unfortunate side-effect. Having received official word that the bread and wine were 'alive', people were dismayed to see their wafers bleeding. Centuries later, it was realized that the occasional red stain came from a bacillus commonly found in stale food, but the good Christians of the thirteenth century had a simpler explanation. It was the Jews. Over the next couple of centuries whole Jewish communities were tortured and burned for their crimes against their Christian neighbours' ceremonial food. The pogroms only began to die out when witches provided an alternative target.

The European pharmacy

The hypocrisy was noticed. The century of Cortez also produced the French essayist Michel de Montaigne, who devoted one of his more famous works to reflections on the subject of cannibalism. After reminding his readers of several culinary crimes committed by the Tupinambas (a tribe indigenous to Brazil), he went on: 'I am not sorry that we notice the barbarous horror of these acts, but I am heartily sorry that, judging their faults rightly, we should be so blind to our own' (see Korn, Radice and Hawes, Bibliography). Montaigne was talking not so much about the Eucharist, as about the growing European habit of using human flesh and blood in medicine. 'Our medical men', he wrote, 'do not flinch from using corpses in many ways, both internally and externally, to cure us' (see Conklin, Bibliography).

This practice had already been noted by the Native Americans, who observed the Spaniards using human fat as a salve for wounds. Medicinal cannibalism had a long history in both Europe and the Mediterranean. The still-warm blood of gladiators who died in the arena was likely to be put on sale and bought by epileptics, and the Roman writer Pliny noted the Egyptian belief in human blood as a cure for leprosy, a belief that persisted, with variations, for most of the next two millennia. An English expert insisted on the blood of two-year-old infants to treat some ailments, while those tending the ailing Louis XI of France were satisfied with any children. His subjects stored this fact in their collective memory, and when, several centuries later, a number of Parisian children went missing, it was generally assumed that the current Louis must have leprosy.

Autocratic kings have traditionally encountered few problems in getting the blood they think they need. Commoners, however, have laws to worry about. One possible legal source of the stuff was the local executioner, who usually owned the rights to his victims' blood.

Executed criminals were a much more common species in past centuries, and a considerable amount of blood could be gathered from the many decapitated bodies. In Denmark, epileptics were said to crowd around the scaffold, cups in hand.

> **The corpse was laid out in good weather for a couple of days before dissection, and then the pieces were sprinkled with myrrh and aloe...it was said to cure just about anything.**

Blood was also used as an ingredient in medicine. Arnald of Villanova, the alchemist credited with the invention of whisky, also invented a cure-all potion with one magic ingredient – the blood of healthy men between twenty-five and thirty. It had to be collected – by what means was not stated – in springtime, and distilled several times with fruit and flower juice. The finished article was guaranteed to keep a dying man going through his final confession.

Human flesh, bones and organs were also used in European medicine. Arthritis, sciatica, infertility, warts and skin blemishes were only a few of the conditions which supposedly responded to the magic of medical cannibalism. Through most of the sixteenth and

Louis XI in robust health: in his later years, his physicians were convinced he could be cured of ill-health by taking the blood of young children

seventeenth centuries, such notions formed the mainstream of European medical thought, and the pharmacies of the day were stocked high with dried and powdered human remains. In London one of the more popular medicines was 'mummy', which was made from an embalmed human body. Young, red-headed men who had died a violent death were considered ideal (but presumably did not present themselves that often). Usually, the corpse was laid out in good weather for a couple of days before dissection, and then the pieces were sprinkled with myrrh and aloe. Soaked in wine and dried in a shady spot, it was said to cure just about anything.

Where did the bodies all come from? Executed criminals were plentiful, but not that plentiful. The answer was importation from Egypt, which for some reason had bodies to spare. Throughout the sixteenth and seventeenth centuries, the Europeans supplied their need for human body parts from across the Mediterranean, while continuing to castigate the newly conquered Native Americans for their terrible addiction to cannibalism.

And hypocrisy was not the Europeans' only crime. They consumed their human flesh as neat,

> **Medicinal cannibalism had a long history in both Europe and the Mediterranean. The still-warm blood of gladiators who died in the arena was likely to be bought by epiliptics, and the Roman writer Pliny noted the Egyptian belief in human blood as a cure for leprosy.**

depersonalized individual prescriptions in pursuit of individual health. Unlike the so-called 'savages', their cannibalism had no social relevance, no religious purpose. They were not keeping the sun in motion across the sky, just creating a new line in commodities.

The passion of the newly converted

By the end of the eighteenth century, the leanings of mainstream medicine began to incline toward the more scientifically minded Galenist school. Natural substances like herbs, leeches and human flesh fell out of medical fashion, leaving Europe essentially cannibal-free. Nineteenth-century colonial administrators and missionaries could set sail for the lands of the heathen with the same intentions and message as Cortez, but with a much clearer conscience. And when they encountered cannibalism their response was much the same. They explained, with a patience steeped in arrogance, that white folks and Christians – the two were, for the moment, considered virtually synonymous – did not hold with that sort of behaviour. And if the indigenous people of Africa, Asia and the Pacific aspired, as they surely must, to the blessings of civilisation, then they had

better put a stop to cannibal practices.

Like Cortez, the new colonialists had found an excuse for their presence; a moral imperative to mask the looting of continents. Indeed, they harped on about cannibalism to such an extent that late twentieth-century anthropologists like William Arens came to the conclusion it had never existed. His failure to appreciate that cannibalism, in the right time and place, could make cultural sense, led him to the conclusion that it was a myth. Cannibalism was 'an impression, an ethnocentric way of looking at the world'; it reflected a 'negative view of non-Western culture' (see Arens, Bibliography). It was, in effect, an essentially racist legend concocted by white colonialists to justify their global hegemony.

A real myth of the time – the benign, close-to-the-earth lifestyle of Native Americans, Tibetans and other Rousseau-esque noble savages – provided sweet confirmation. How could peoples with such great philosophies and fashion sense be cannibals?

Historical tradition of cannibalism

A better way of correcting the European identification of cannibalism with skin colour was already at hand. By the end of

A better way of correcting the European identification of cannibalism with skin colour was already at hand. By the end of the twentieth century, new technology was supplying a steady stream of evidence to the contrary.

the twentieth century, new technology was supplying a steady stream of archaeological evidence to the contrary. Europe's long history of cannibalism was there to be read in the ancient bones.

Living bone tissue is soft, and heals with time. Dead bone tissue does not so much break as shatter. So bones with clean breaks that have not healed are likely to have been broken around the time of death. There are not that many explanations for such breaks, but processing a carcass for food is clearly one of them.

The archaeological dig at Gran Dolina in northern Spain has provided more than

The heyday of medicinal cannibalism might be past, but 'fringe cannibalism' benefits like blood transfusion and organ transplants are only eschewed by the Jehovah's Witnesses.

three-quarters of all human remains dating between 100,000 and 1.5 million years ago. One group of fossilized remains dug up in the mid-1990s was particularly revealing. The bones of the six individuals concerned all had the sort of cut marks you would find on butchered, dismembered and filleted animals. Indeed, animal bones with such marks were also found mixed in with the human ones, suggesting that both were discarded food. Some of the larger bones had clearly been broken over some sort of anvil, presumably for extraction of the nutritious marrow. Last but not least, there was clear evidence of other decent-sized animal prey. If, as seemed more than likely, the humans had been cannibalized, it had not been from necessity.

Another dig, in 1986, at Gough's Cave in Britain's Cheddar Gorge revealed a similar pattern. Another group of human bones, this one only 12,000 years old, bore the same cuts suggesting butchery and dismemberment. The cut marks on one skull clearly showed where a right-handed person had cut upwards with a flint tool to remove the flesh. As at Gran Dolina, human remains were mixed in with similarly processed animal remains.

A third and final example cropped up, also in the mid-1980s, at Fontbregoua

Cave in south-eastern France. Six humans – two small children, one youth, two young adults and an older adult – had died as part of a single event, and the animal bones mixed in with their own seemed to rule out famine. Cut marks on the skulls of both humans and animals show that both were skinned, which is highly suggestive. Burial rituals involving the skinning of humans are not unheard of, but animals? Hardly the stuff of ritual. Once again, cannibalism was the logical explanation. Europeans, it now seems certain, had been eating each other for thousands of years.

Taboo or not taboo?

Less than two hundred years ago cannibals and cannibalism were not that hard to find. Less than four hundred years ago a wide range of human parts were on sale in the pharmacies of early modern Europe. Now, though, in the globalized world of the twenty-first century, cultural or duty cannibalism has all but vanished. A newly discovered tribe with regrettable eating habits is sometimes dragged into the dubious light of the 'modern' world, but these newly discovered cultures are few and far between. These days it would appear that people only eat each other out of desperation or desire.

So why has duty cannibalism gone the way of the dodo? The colonialists and missionaries were correct in thinking they stopped it, but the only light the locals saw was that of the approaching gunship. Threatened, coerced and bribed, the Third World fell into line with varying degrees of enthusiasm. And as the years went by, there was little reason to look back. Very few developing-world cannibals ate their own people, and then only in tightly regulated circumstances. Most of the relevant cultures were fighting continual wars with each other to gain the necessary victims, a practice which the international community increasingly came to frown on, with or without the cannibalism. Such wars, in any case, could only really be sustained when the enemy could be demonized, dehumanized or both; they became much harder to arrange when the chiefs were all riding the same globalized gravy trains, all watching the same globalized soaps. And there was no doubt that cannibalism inhibited economic development – corporate scouts who heard rumours of strange, taboo practices were unlikely to recommend the location for major investment. The Third World gave up cannibalism, but only because Judaeo-Christian Europe and North America insisted they do so.

And why is the developed world so opposed to the practice? The heyday of medicinal cannibalism might be past, but 'fringe cannibalism' benefits like blood transfusions and organ transplants are only eschewed by the Jehovah's Witnesses. Yet eating human flesh is a gigantic no-no, the sort of behaviour that, in normal circumstances, is utterly beyond the pale. Why has this happened? And why the strange insistence on calling cannibalism the 'oldest taboo', when it is clearly anything but?

These days it would appear that people only eat each other out of desperation or desire.

Some claim that the evolution of the Judaeo-Christian mindset – and, in particular, the notion of the Last Judgement – makes it essential that the body remains whole beyond death. In this light, cutting up dead bodies for food becomes every bit as reprehensible as killing a live person with the same object in mind. Both constitute murder, and murder, more or less everywhere, was and is taboo.

3: Cannibalism And Disasters

Lost at sea

The second obvious reason for cannibalism has been the lack of an alternative source of nourishment; throughout history, people with no other food have eaten other people. In times of peace and normal plenty, it is quite difficult to find places on earth where nothing else is available, but an open boat in the middle of the ocean has often been one of them. You might think that fish would fill the long spaces between meals, but, for whatever reasons – lack of bait, lack of line, rough seas, indifferent fish or incompetent fishers – they rarely have. Flying fish have sometimes obliged by flying into the open boat, but in most of the famous circumstances described below, the only thing crew and/or passengers had to eat was each other. The good guys usually waited for someone to die, or at least held an honest drawing of lots. The bad guys simply murdered.

The *Nottingham Galley*

The clipper ship *Nottingham Galley* left Boston for London in early December 1710 with a crew of fourteen and a cargo of butter and cheese. Making its way up the coast of Maine and Nova Scotia it soon encountered rough seas, and on the night of 11 December ran into a large rock some twelve miles offshore. As the boat began breaking up, the crew jumped overboard, and by something of a miracle all reached the relative safety of the rock.

Morning found the *Nottingham Galley* transformed into driftwood; twelve miles of rough and frigid sea divided the rock-bound crew from safety and sustenance. Seaweed, the odd mussel, and a few lumps of washed-up cheese were the only items left on the menu. Unable to get a fire started, the crew soon fell prey to frostbite and extreme hunger. Thoughts of cannibalism apparently surfaced in the first few days, but it took almost three weeks, and the death of four men, before action was taken. Seeing no alternative, the captain ordered the dismemberment of the fourth fatality – a plump carpenter. The head, hands and feet were cut off, the rest of the body skinned and cut into strips. Three of the ten survivors could not bring themselves to eat their former shipmate on this first day, but fell into line on the second. Wrapping the strips in seaweed made them more palatable.

The carpenter kept them going until a rescue ship arrived on 4 January. Back in London, the crew openly admitted what

Gericault's *The Raft of the Medusa* controversially depicted – on a scale normally reserved for grand art – a shocking shipwreck and a Government scandal

they had done. 'It was no Sin, since God was pleased to take him out of the world and that we had not laid violent hands on him,' one crew member said (See Korn, Radice and Hawes, Bibliography). No one seemed to blame them for it, and then, as now, there was no law against cannibalism as such. The Captain's career hardly suffered – he soon secured an appointment in the diplomatic service, as British Consul in Flanders.

The *Peggy*

Half a century later, in October 1765, an American boat set out across the Atlantic in the opposite direction. The *Peggy* had a crew of ten, one of whom was an African slave. The ship's hold was full of kegs of wine and brandy.

The *Peggy* did not hit a rock, but it might as well have done. A storm raged for a couple of weeks, destroyed the ship's masts and sails, and left it drifting helplessly in the mid-Atlantic. The ship's already scanty food supplies soon ran out. The sailors had a few drinks to get their situation in perspective, and then had a few more. After consuming the ship's cat, a couple of pet pigeons, the available candles and all the leather they could find, their attention settled on – you guessed it – the African slave. A drawing of lots was decided, approved by the captain, and in all likelihood fixed: the slave was shot. Some of the meat was cooked for immediate consumption, some pickled for later.

What followed is not clear. According to one account, one of the seamen ate the slave's liver raw, and went mad as a result. According to most accounts, the whole crew were not in that much of a better state, having drunk the entire ship's cargo and copious amounts of sea-water. Once the slave had been consumed, a second drawing of lots was ordered, and, in the absence of a suitable scapegoat, was fairly conducted. The ship's most popular sailor drew the short straw, and was given a twelve-hour reprieve out of sympathy. A rescue ship appeared on the horizon with a couple of hours to go.

Taken to Dartmouth in Devon, the survivors encountered no more criticism than their predecessors on the *Nottingham Galley*. The fiction of fair lottery was not challenged – in 1766 the fact that a black man's life was worth as much as a white man's was an opinion held only by a few.

La Méduse

In June 1816 the French frigate *La Méduse* (Medusa) sailed for the port of St Louis in the West African colony of Senegal, with a complement of around 400 – crew, soldiers and would-be settlers. Thanks to the incompetence of its captain, the ship ran aground on reefs off the north-west African coast and had to be abandoned. The six available lifeboats could only hold 250, so a raft was constructed for the remaining 150. By the time they were loaded, the raft sat three feet below the surface, its passengers up to their waists in water.

The captain and senior officers grabbed places in the lifeboats, claiming that their nautical skills were necessary for tugging the laden raft to safety. They then reached the conclusion that the dead weight of their fellow humans was holding them back unnecessarily, and cut the raft loose.

There was still no sign of rescue, and by the sixth day hunger, thirst, exposure and executions for wine-stealing had reduced the living to twenty-eight. Of these, thirteen looked doomed, and the other fifteen...decided that an immediate cull would help...

The 150 were left with no food, a few casks of wine, and no means of moving or steering their barely-floating platform.

Twenty died on the first night, either swept overboard or drowned with their feet caught in the planking. A lot of wine was consumed during the following day, and, as night fell, people started fighting for the safer positions at the centre of the raft. One man lost his mind completely, and started hacking at the ropes holding the raft together. An attempt by junior officers to subdue him quickly escalated into a full-scale battle, with sabres and knives striking out in the dark at anything that moved. By morning sixty-five people were dead, with most of the survivors carrying wounds of varying seriousness.

Perhaps sobered by the carnage, they tried fishing, but either their lines got trapped under the raft or their bayonets proved too slow for the prey. After chewing a while on their leather belts and hats, they finally acceded to the obvious and started cutting up the plentiful supply of corpses. According to one of the few survivors, ship's surgeon Savigny, some

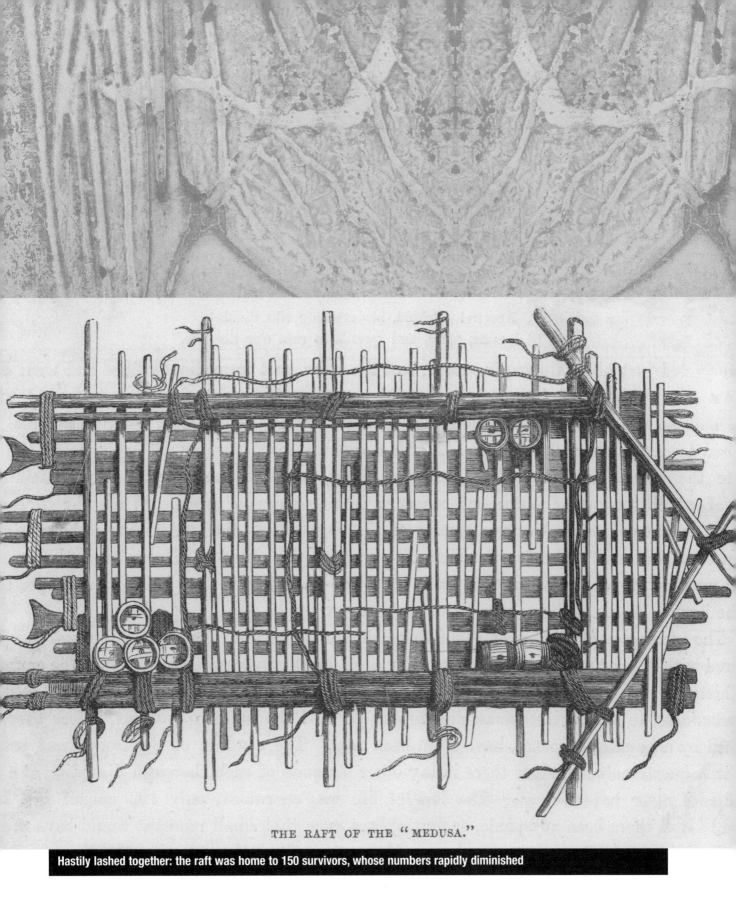

THE RAFT OF THE "MEDUSA."

Hastily lashed together: the raft was home to 150 survivors, whose numbers rapidly diminished

'refused to touch the horrible food' (*The Times*, 17 September 1816), but on the following day some of the junior officers managed to make it more palatable by conjuring a cooking fire out of gunpowder, dry rags and a tinderbox.

There was still no sign of rescue, and by the sixth day hunger, thirst, exposure and executions for wine-stealing had reduced the living to twenty-eight. Of these, thirteen looked doomed, and the other fifteen, 'after long deliberation', decided that an immediate cull would help conserve the remaining supplies of wine. Those deemed not fit were thrown overboard. 'We averted our eyes', Savigny wrote later, 'and shed tears of blood over the fate of these unhappy creatures' (The *Times*, 17.9.1816).

A week later, the survivors were picked up. Savigny and another man, ship's engineer Corréard, tried to get compensation from the French government. They claimed, quite correctly, that the whole tragedy had been set in motion by the incompetence and cowardice of the naval ship's captain. The French government refused to accept that the well-born captain and officers of the ship had done wrong, and hounded Savigny and Corréard from government service. They had their revenge by writing a book about the affair, and one of their readers, Théodore Géricault, turned it into one of Romantic art's most famous paintings. His vast canvas *The Raft of the Medusa* adorns the Louvre in Paris.

The *Essex*

The Nantucket whaler *Essex* was preserved for posterity in another way – its story turned up in Herman Melville's *Moby-Dick* as the *Pequod*. The ship left its home port in August 1819, and by November 1821 was whaling in the vast expanses of the south-eastern Pacific. Three whales had been killed when a fourth fought back with devastating effect, ramming the whaler and staving in her bow. The crew had time to launch their three lifeboats and load them with bread, fresh water and material for making sails. Afraid that they might end up on islands populated by cannibals they even remembered to take muskets and powder. In the panic of the moment they seem to have forgotten only one thing – the charts and navigational instruments they needed to find any sort of landfall.

They gradually consumed the bread, reducing the daily ration to almost nothing as the days and weeks went by. They finished the water and started drinking their own urine. A month after setting out they came ashore on the uninhabited Henderson Island, which proved depressingly lacking in food or water. Sailing east once more, the small flotilla was separated by a storm. The two boats under the captain's command continued in an easterly direction, their crews suffering more and more acutely from malnutrition, dehydration and sunburn. On 20 January, two months to the day since the whale had sunk the *Essex*, a black crewman named Lawson Thomas died. The other crewmen used the skills learnt on whale carcasses to cut him up. They made a fire in the bottom of one boat, roasted his flesh and organs, and divided them up for consumption.

Over the next eight days three more sailors – two black and one white – died. All were cooked and eaten. Seven men remained in the two boats, only one of them black. During that night the boat containing him and two white sailors disappeared, never to be seen again. In the remaining boat, Captain Pollard and three young sailors – one of them his

The clipper *Essex*, a whaler in the south-eastern Pacific. A dangerous occupation, whaling was the cause of many wrecked ships

Afraid that they might end up on islands populated by cannibals they even remembered to take muskets and powder. In the panic of the moment they seem to have forgotten one thing – the charts and navigational instruments...

cousin, Owen Coffin – consumed what was left of the last corpse. By February 6 the meat was all gone, and they drew lots for who should die to feed the other three. Coffin lost. The captain offered to take his place, but Coffin refused, and was duly killed. On 23 February the three survivors were finally rescued by another whaler.

Reaching home in August, they discovered that the crewmen in the third boat had also cannibalized their dead in order to survive. For Pollard, one dreadful task remained. He had to tell his aunt that he had killed and eaten her son.

Sketched by Mr Stephens, the mate, the dinghy that the survivors of the *Mignonette* survived on for 21 days

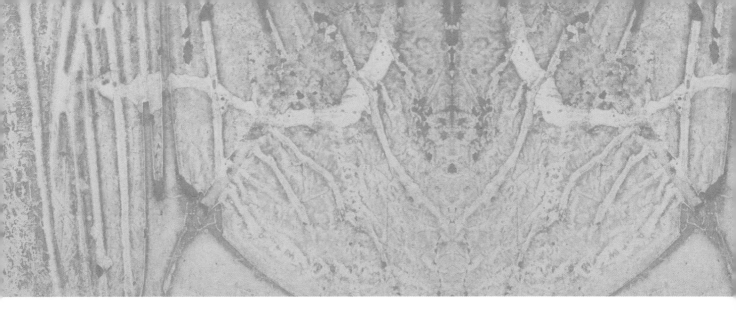

The *Mignonette*

The *Mignonette* case was interesting because the legality of high seas cannibalism – the 'custom of the sea' as it was now being called with minimal irony – was, for the first time, brought into question.

The boat was a 52-foot yacht which an Australian had purchased in England with home delivery in mind. He paid a Captain Dudley £200 to get the ship to Australia, and Dudley hired two seamen (Stephens and Brooks) and a seventeen-year-old cabin boy (Richard Parker) to make up the crew. They left Southampton on 19 May 1884 and made relatively good time down the coasts of Spain and Africa, crossing the equator in mid-June.

The South Atlantic proved less amenable, and one in a series of storms finally sealed the fate of the *Mignonette*. The crew damaged the bottom of the dinghy in their rush to launch it, and found themselves with only two cans of vegetables in a boat that required constant bailing. Rain was their only source of drinking water.

By the sixteenth day they were all starving, and the cabin boy was delirious from drinking seawater. Captain Dudley put it to the other two that killing and eating the boy was their only chance of survival. Brooks refused to have anything to do with the plan, but Dudley and Stephens – both of whom had families – agreed to kill the boy if the following day brought neither rain nor sight of sail. It did not. Dudley slit the boy's throat, allegedly after praying for forgiveness, and the corpse was eaten.

Rain fell constantly until, a week later, another ship, the German freighter *Montezuma*, appeared on the horizon. On their long journey back to England, the three men must have considered concocting a less damning explanation for Richard Parker's death, but on arrival in Falmouth they simply told the truth. All three were arraigned before magistrates on murder charges. Brooks was discharged but the other two were sent for trial in a blaze of publicity. Public opinion, for the most part, was on their side, and a public appeal paid most of their legal costs.

Their defence counsel produced a

The *Mignonette* case was interesting because the legality of high seas cannibalism...was, for the first time, brought into question.

mishmash of points in mitigation. In desperate conditions, he claimed, laws were irrelevant. In such desperate conditions as these, he argued, individuals were no longer responsible for their actions – a precursor of today's 'while-the-balance-of-mind-is-disturbed' temporary insanity plea. He also seemed, at one point, to be arguing for the general proposition that humans were weak, and that not much more could be expected of them, particularly in desperate straits.

Once the biscuit-can boiler was half-full of flesh, they covered it with salt and set a fire, using the flares that remained to ignite the fuel.

His best point, however, was that the killing of Richard Parker had benefited the majority; that one man – or boy – had died so that three others could live.

The judge obviously did not like the way things were going, and took the decision out of the jury's hands. The case was moved to another court, with five judges presiding. They did not think much of the 'necessity' defence either. If such a defence were allowed, they pointed out, then a man dying of hunger would be justified in stealing food. Not according to my moral code, they all agreed. Dudley and Stephens were sentenced to death, and the point was made. Once it had sunk in, the Crown was able to step in with a reprieve, and reduce the sentences to six months.

The *Dumaru*

The *Dumaru* was a wooden steamship built, rather badly, in Portland, Oregon. In order to save money, unseasoned green timbers were used in the construction, and unseasoned green timbers, as every sailor knew, were apt to warp in the tropics. The *Dumaru*, indeed, seemed cursed from the very beginning. On launching, it was sent down the Willamette river slipway at such a speed that it crashed into the far bank.

The story of the ship and its last crew was told with melodramatic relish by Lowell Thomas. He was ghost-writing for Fritz Harmon, one of the engineers unfortunate enough to serve aboard the *Dumaru*. The ship made its final voyage in 1918, and most of the crew, according to Harmon, were either hardened Bolsheviks or men evading a spell in the French trenches.

Somewhat ironically for the latter, the ship they had signed on to was carrying explosives across the Pacific. It creaked its way westward from San Francisco, until, an hour or so out of Guam, it ran into an electrical storm. A bolt of lightning sparked an uncontrollable fire, and the crew scrambled for the two lifeboats and one life raft. They managed to put enough distance between themselves and the doomed *Dumaru* before it exploded, but that, for some of them, was the end of the good news. One lifeboat reached land and the raft was picked up, but the second lifeboat was left to drift in the western Pacific for twenty-four long days.

Its occupants seem to have divided along class lines, with the outnumbered but better-armed officers confronting a mixed

bag of mutinous ratings, 'Filipinos' and other characters seemingly out of a bad movie. After several days without food, one of the latter, a character named George the Greek, led a mutiny. The chief engineer had just died, and the decision was taken to eat him. Thomas/Harmon takes up the story: 'Hardened to suffering and seeing death at its worst, still we were not left entirely without feeling. I was one of several who had to look away when the Greek removed the head and placed other parts in the biscuit-can boiler. He scoffed at our timidity and called out to us to witness his act, asking in his broken English if we were chickens or men' (see Lowell, Bibliography). Once the biscuit-can boiler was half-full of flesh, they covered it with salt and set a fire, using the flares that remained to ignite what fuel there was. The flames lit up the boat. 'The Greek and the small wolfish Filipinos squatting about the fire as they waited for the contents of the can to boil did not make a pleasant sight…' (see Lowell, Bibliography).

Perhaps dulled by a good meal, the Greek and his companions were overpowered during the night, and the natural order was restored. Faced with the Chief Engineer's remains the officer class

discovered some wolfishness of their own. The idea of the mutineers, it seemed, had not been entirely misguided. 'We decided to go right on with what the Greek had started, for it was mutually agreed after a consultation among all the other white hands that it was the only possible means of saving our lives, and for our comrades it was a fate not much worse than to be eaten by sharks' (see Lowell, Bibliography).

What remained in the can was boiled into a broth and served up in enamel cups and a wooden bailer. 'The salt in the seawater in which the flesh was boiled was absorbed by the flesh, leaving the broth free from salt and not unpleasant to taste. The flesh was like tough veal. The cups and bailer were filled and passed to each man until the can was empty. It was both food and drink to us. It put new life in our bodies' (see Lowell, Bibliography).

The next to die was an Hawaiian with the improbable name of Honolulu Pete. Since another man, Ole Heikland, seemed near to death, it was immediately suggested that he be fed the blood from Pete's still-warm body. The head was removed, the swiftly thickening blood transferred to an empty kerosene can and diluted with water. A cup was taken to

There were 110 would-be escapees from Vietnam on board...The organizers had reckoned on a maximum of six days to reach the coast, and had economically catered for one day less. On the third day the junk's engine broke down.

Heikland, and forced through his lips. Asked whether he felt any better, he said 'Give me more.' After this testimonial, everyone had a cup.

Honolulu Pete followed the Chief Engineer into the biscuit-can boiler. They took turns cutting him up while the head 'rolled about in the bottom of the boat'. The arrival of daylight offered a memorably gruesome sight – 'a headless body, half-leaning, half-sitting against the side of the boat; without arms and with the flesh removed from the legs, it had the appearance of a half-made scarecrow, for the feet were still in the shoes' (see Lowell, Bibliography).

When Thomas/Harmon eventually published their account they were accused of exaggeration, but the story, with much the same details, can also be found in the records section of the US Navy Department Intelligence Division in Washington, DC.

In the South China Sea

Towards the end of May 1988, an already leaking, forty-five foot motorized junk slipped down one of the Mekong Delta channels and out into the South China Sea. There were 110 would-be escapees from Vietnam on board. Each had paid an ounce of gold for the one-way trip to Malaysia.

The organizers had reckoned on a maximum of six days to reach the Malaysian coast, and had economically catered for one day less. On the third day the junk's engine broke down. On the fifth day the food and water ran out. Like many of its predecessors in these pages, the junk was left to the mercy of wind and current.

Unlike many of its predecessors, the junk was not left to its own devices, though it might as well have been. The stricken craft's first encounter with potential assistance came five days later – a Japanese freighter passed within a hundred yards of the now-desperate refugees. Twelve of them leapt into the sea and swam towards the freighter, which just kept on going. The twelve were all drowned.

The next meeting involved a US naval vessel, the 8,600 ton amphibious transport *Dubuque*. What exactly happened during this encounter became a matter of serious dispute. The American ship was apparently heading, on an urgent mission, for the far-distant Persian Gulf. Captain Balian later claimed that he had not gone aboard the junk, but that the junk's passengers were in 'relatively good shape'. He also denied that one of his junior officers had promised the refugees that a rescue ship would be arriving in two days.

Those refugees who survived told a different story. According to Dinh Thuong

After the Vietnam War, over one million refugees fled Vietnam, Cambodia and Laos. Dubbed 'boat people', unscrupulous middlemen put the refugees' lives in danger by providing unseaworthy vessels and rarely arranging legal entry to countries

With very few – if any – regulations on sea-going vessels in areas such as south-east Asia, it is inevitable that disasters like that which happened in May 1988 in the Mekong Delta can only happen again

Hai, one of their number died during the two-hour encounter with the *Dubuque*, and was thrown overboard in full view of the American ship. Indeed, several American sailors were seen taking photos of the body in the water. 'There was no doubt the Americans knew how desperate we were' (see Askenasy, Bibliography), Dinh said later.

They certainly did not show it. After

handing over six cases of tinned meat and twelve gallons of fresh water the Americans sailed off, without even bothering to check whether they could help with the broken-down engine. It seems probable that US naval captains in the area were under instructions not to pick up refugees, but at least four other American ships had done so that very same year. Their captains seem to have put

common humanity first: Captain Balian was apparently made of 'sterner' stuff.

On the twice-scorned junk, one refugee, a former South Vietnamese Red Beret named Phung Quang Minh, took charge. Reasoning that the new food and water supplies only had to last two days, he rationed them out accordingly. When the promised assistance failed to show, the refugees were left with nothing.

They began to die at regular intervals. Phung later said that they all decided on the twenty-eighth day at sea 'to use the dying to help the living' (see Askenasy, Bibliography). He also admitted to killing at least one refugee for food, a thirty-year-old named Dao Cu Cuong. A twelve year-old boy, Pham Quy, was also murdered, and perhaps two others. 'All the passengers were forced to eat', Dinh said. 'We were told we had to eat to stay strong, and if we did not we would be next' (see Askenasy, Bibliography).

When the junk was finally rescued by Philippine fishermen on 28 June, only fifty-two of the refugees were still alive. Phung and nine others were arrested and jailed, but the Philippine authorities soon realized that they had no jurisdiction over crimes allegedly committed in international waters. Phung himself was unrepentant. 'I was only a man who was thinking more clearly than the others,' he said. 'I had to do what I did to keep all the people living. I had no other choice' (see Askenasy, Bibliography). The nagging question remains – why was it necessary to kill at least two of the refugees, when so many corpses were already available?

Captain Balian had certainly been confronted with a clear choice, and the US Navy decided he had chosen wrongly. He was court-martialled for 'dereliction of duty'.

Lost on land

Finding yourself lost on land without a source of nourishment is probably more unlucky – and more difficult to do – than finding yourself lost at sea in a similar predicament. Few places on dry land are utterly devoid of food or water, and those who choose to visit them tend to pack accordingly. To end up in such an unforgiving wilderness without the necessary supplies you have to be spectacularly unlucky or misguidedly ignorant.

The Donner party

The eighty-seven California-bound migrants in George Donner's wagon train were a bit of both. They were unlucky with the advice they received – a 'short cut' through the Wasatch Mountains cost them weeks they did not have – and they were recklessly stupid to attempt a crossing of the Sierra Nevada mountains so late in the year. In the event, fifteen of the twenty-three wagons which left Missouri had reached one of two camps 6,000 feet up in the mountains by the beginning of November 1846. Then the snow started,

immobilizing the wagons. An attempt was made to continue on foot, but abandoned after four days of struggling through chest-deep snow.

The first camp, on the shores of Truckee Lake, housed around sixty of the seventy-nine travellers who had survived the passage of the Wasatch Mountains and the Great Salt Desert. They built rough log cabins to protect them from the elements. Five miles back down the trail, the other twenty or so travellers, who included the families of George Donner and his brother, made do with lean-tos covered in wagon canvas and buffalo hides. Both groups were already short of food. They killed and roasted the oxen which had pulled their wagons, but by mid-November it was clear they would starve without outside help.

In the second half of November, two parties from the larger camp tried to reach the summit on foot, but both were forced back by exhaustion. On 16 December, a third group of twelve men and five women set out on crudely-manufactured snowshoes. Two men turned back on the second day, but the others pushed on towards the summit, driven half-mad by hunger, cold and the effects of altitude. By Christmas Day three had died; the

Five miles down the trail, the other twenty or so travellers, who included the families of George Donner and his brother, made do with lean-tos covered in wagon canvas and buffalo hides. Both groups were already short of food. They killed and roasted the oxen...but it was clear they would starve without outside help.

Covered wagons were a perilous means of transport – slow and cumbersome, journeys took time

The original tracks left in the desert surface from the ill-fated Donner-Reed party of 1847

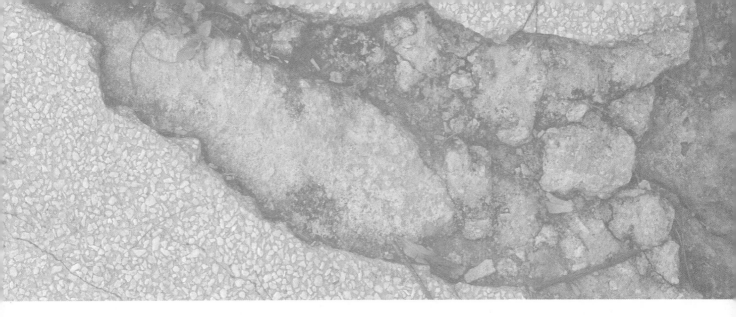

following day, a fourth followed. Stuck in a snowstorm, they roasted the fourth fatality over an open fire, and all tucked in. Their strength renewed, the travellers cut up, cooked and packed four other bodies (three of the original casualties and one new one). Five women and five men were left, including the two Indians sent from Sutter's Fort in October to help guide the whole party across the mountains.

By New Year's Day the food was all gone. Of the three white men, the quasi-deranged Foster favoured killing the Indians, Fosdick was too far gone to decide, and Eddy was sufficiently outraged to warn the putative prey. The Indians left, and Fosdick's death provided – despite his wife's pleadings – an alternative source of food. A few days later, with Fosdick half-consumed, the party overtook the exhausted Indians. Ignoring the others' protests, Foster shot them both. The party split up. Foster and two of the women took the Indian corpses to eat, Eddy and the other three women took what was left of Fosdick. Ten days later

> **At the Truckee Lake camp a half-eaten corpse and several half-chewed bones littered the snow...the man who came to greet them was carrying a human leg.**

both parties reeled into Johnson's Ranch, the first white settlement in California, faces streaked with human blood.

By this time the occupants of the two camps had eaten their dogs, their belts and the hides which formed the roofs of their cabins. But they had not yet started eating each other. When the first rescue party reached the camps in mid-February the emaciated corpses in the snow were still whole. Twenty-four of the fifty-six survivors were deemed fit to travel, and these were escorted across the pass by their rescuers. The other thirty-two were left, without fresh supplies, to wait for another rescue party. When this finally arrived on 1 March it was confronted with a less wholesome picture. At the Truckee Lake camp a half-eaten corpse and several half-chewed bones littered the snow; at the other camp the man who came to greet them was carrying a human leg. Jacob Donner had died and been cut up, the rescuers were told. His wife had refused to eat him, but had fed him to his children.

Another party set out for the west, only

Lewis Keseberg had definitely strayed across the border which separates cannibalism-through-desperation from cannibalism-through-desire...he was widely considered a murderer, but no one could prove it.

to find itself caught up in the worst snowstorm of the winter. With all its food gone and people dying by the day, both rescuees and rescuers were reduced to consuming one dead woman and two dead children. The eleven who survived were apparently too shocked to discuss the experience.

The German Lewis Keseberg would show no such reticence. Left behind with the Donners, the unofficial leader of the Truckee Lake Camp had slipped the bounds of human restraint. He took a four-year-old boy to bed with him, and announced the following morning that the boy had died in the night. His fellow campers were dismayed to find the boy already hung up for butchering.

This indiscretion got him banned from the third rescue party's trip to safety. Unfortunately, Mrs Donner, her dead husband's four-year-old nephew and the elderly Lavinia Murphy were also left behind. Two fit survivors were also left to

ensure fair play, but they soon disappeared with all the possessions they could carry. When the fourth and final rescue party arrived at Truckee Lake on 17 April, they found only Keseberg. There were two cauldrons of human blood in his cabin, and fresh liver sizzling in the pan.

He denied killing anyone. Mrs Donner, he said, had wandered off into the snow and died of exposure. 'Some of her is there,' he told his rescuers, pointing to the frying pan. 'I've eaten the rest,' he added somewhat gratuitously. 'She was the best I ever tasted' (see Marriner, Bibliography).

Over the next few days, as they prepared for departure, the rescuers could not help noticing the amount of frozen horse and ox-meat still littering the snow. 'Why did you not eat that?' they asked.

'I tried them,' Keseberg said, 'but they were too dry for my taste. Human liver and lungs are far more tasty. And as for human brains, well, they make the best soup of all' (see Marriner, Bibliography).

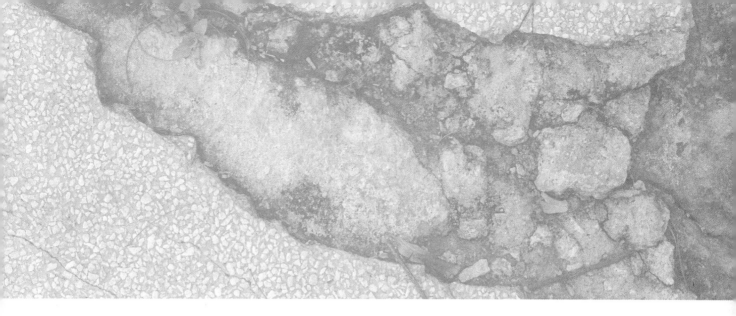

George Donner, the rescuers remembered, had been found with a hole in his skull.

Lewis Keseberg had definitely strayed across the border which separates cannibalism-through-desperation from cannibalism-through-desire. Back in what passed for civilization, he was widely considered a murderer, but no one could prove it, and he successfully sued one accuser for slander. He probably put the derisory one dollar damages towards his next project – a steakhouse.

The Franklin expedition

If the members of the Donner party stumbled blindly into their wilderness of snow and ice, Sir John Franklin headed into his with his eyes wide open. And while Donner and his companions were having their winter to remember in the Sierra Nevada, Franklin and his group, who had set out a year earlier, were already on the missing list.

There were 129 officers and men on the two ships which left Greenland on 12 July 1845. The point of this expedition – and of many others – was to find a short cut between the Atlantic

> **'Some of her is there,' he told his rescuers, pointing to the frying pan. 'I've eaten the rest,' he added, somewhat gratuitously.**

and the Pacific. The potential benefits of this elusive 'North-West Passage' remain something of a mystery, but the determination to find it was clearly an abiding obsession. The Franklin Expedition was equipped with state-of-the-art Victoriana: iron-plated, steam-heated ships; desalinators for turning sea water into fresh water; food packed in revolutionary new containers made of tin; some of the earliest cameras. It was last seen on 26 July by two whaling ships in Baffin Bay.

In the ensuing years, search party after search party ventured north in search of a trace. Finally, in 1859, a pile of discarded equipment was found on King William Island in the heart of the Canadian Arctic. There were also two skeletons and an explanatory message from Franklin's deputy, Francis Crozier. The expedition's boats, he wrote, had been trapped in sea-ice for almost two years. During that time Franklin and twenty-three others had died. In April 1845, the remaining 105 men had abandoned the ship and headed south, hoping to cross the narrow strait

Members of the Arctic expedition led by Sir John Franklin. The expedition was beleaguered by thick ice: Franklin died

in June 1847, and most of the team also died from starvation

which separates King William Island from the Canadian mainland. Once across, there was the minor matter of a thousand-mile walk to safety. None had survived. The remains of twenty or so men were found along the intended route southwards, but the rest had left no trace.

Their tragedy had not gone unwitnessed, however, and according to the Inuit who witnessed it, the white men had started eating their dead when the food ran out. Of course no one in Victorian Britain was likely to take the word of 'sex-mad savages' who lived in igloos, not, that is, until a certain Dr Rae was called in by the Admiralty to examine the evidence. Rae, much to the dismay of his employers, confirmed the Inuit account. 'From the mutilated contents of the corpses and the contents of the kettles,' he wrote, 'it is evident that our wretched countrymen had been driven to the last resource – cannibalism' (see Korn, Radice and Hawes, Bibliography).

The public refused to believe it, and the matter was laid to rest. More than a century later, bones with tell-tale cuts were discovered on one of the Franklin sites on King William Island. Alternative explanations to cannibalism were offered, but further findings at a brand new site in Erebus Bay were even more conclusive. Analysis of the bones found there, and of the cut-marks they bore, were 'consistent with defleshing or removal of muscle tissue. Evidence for decapitation', the report continued, was 'suggestive but not conclusive' (see Keenleyside, Bibliography).

Martin Hartwell

The story of the Franklin Expedition and its descent into cannibalism was no doubt familiar to Martin Hartwell, who worked as a bush pilot in the Canadian Arctic. Hartwell was 47 years old in November 1972, when he was asked to undertake an emergency flight from Cambridge Bay to the hospital at Yellowknife, some 600 miles to the south. A fourteen-year-old Inuit boy named David Kootook had all the symptoms of acute appendicitis, and his 28-year-old aunt Neemee Nulliayok was suffering complications in her eighth month of pregnancy. A 27-year-old English nurse named Judith Hill was coming with them.

Hartwell only had a VFR (Visual Flight Rules) licence, which prohibited him from flying unless he could guarantee sight of the ground. Strictly speaking, he should have refused to take them. Understandably – and unfortunately for all concerned – he decided that the condition of the two Inuit justified a flouting of the regulations.

His plane was soon enveloped in low clouds and falling snow. Darkness came all too soon, and radio contact proved intermittent. He was already 200 miles off course when the plane crashed into a hillside.

Judith Hill died instantly, Neemee Nulliayok a few hours later from the broken neck she had sustained. Hartwell had two broken ankles, a shattered knee and a badly injured hand. Only David Kootook was unharmed.

Hartwell set the boy to work building a shelter, and taught him how to set traps.

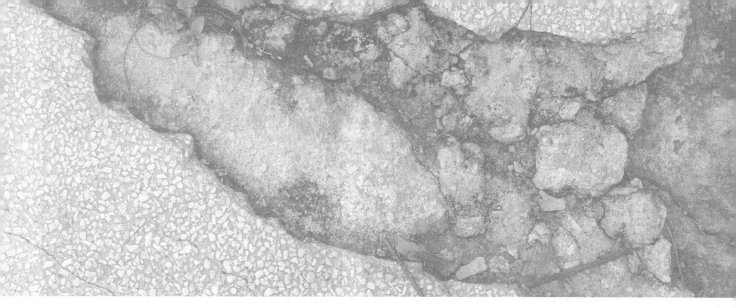

They had what seemed a reasonable supply of emergency rations – cans of corned beef, packets of dried soup, Oxo cubes, rice and powdered potato, a few ounces of raisins – and reasonable hopes of being found before it all ran out. Twenty days later, it had run out. Hartwell's injuries and the waist-deep snow ruled out movement.

A vegetarian in normal times, he made what seemed the obvious suggestion. 'I asked the boy if he would eat human flesh, since it was the only thing we had around. He said "Shut up, I am going to die now."' (see Marriner, Bibliography).

And die he did on the following day. Hartwell managed to make himself a mouthful of soup from lichen and snow, but knew he could never make enough. 'There was no way out but to eat human flesh and this I did,' he said later. For the next eight days he subsisted on the body of Judith Hill. 'The worst thing was to take the first bite,' he said. 'The horror of what I was doing did not bother me after that' (see Marriner, Bibliography).

It was no longer horrible, but it still felt deeply wrong. He lost all faith in God, and fully expected condemnation – even execution – if he was ever rescued. Though cannibalising the dead seemed the only rational course, David Kootook's refusal to take the same way out brought everything into question.

After Hartwell's rescue, the controversy centred, not on cannibalism, but on his flouting of the flight regulations. He eventually sold his story to pay his lawyer, but only with the greatest reluctance. He had, he said, no desire to 'cause distress to the relatives of those who had died' (see Marriner, Bibliography).

Hartwell carried on flying, but knew he would never be the same again. Asked what he would do if the same situation recurred, he had no doubts. 'I would say: Shut up I am going to die now – like David did' (see Marriner, Bibliography).

The Uruguayan rugby tour

There have been four famous examples of cannibalism while lost on land, and by an extraordinary twist of fate they came in overlapping pairs. Just as the Donner party and the Franklin expedition both succumbed in 1846, so Martin Hartwell shared his moment of unwanted fame with a planeload of Uruguayans stranded high in the Andes Mountains in the final months of 1972.

The plane in question was a Uruguayan Air Force Fairchild F-277. It had been chartered by the Old Christians rugby club, who were hoping to repeat their successful playing trip to Chile the previous summer. The charter was not cheap and the team had managed to fill the rest of the seats with family members, friends and other supporters. The rugby club had first been formed from graduates of the exclusive Stella Maris school, and those who climbed aboard the Fairchild were mostly representatives of their country's social elite. They included two of the President's nephews, and the sons of a prominent heart specialist and well-known painter.

The forty-five passengers and crew left early in the morning of 12 October, expecting to reach Santiago early that afternoon. The air above the Andean passes is notorious for its turbulence, and the weather reports that morning convinced the pilots that a twenty-four hour stopover in Mendoza was necessary. They took off again early in the following afternoon, aiming to cross the mountain barrier via the Planchon Pass. An hour after take-off the co-pilot, who was flying the plane, told Santiago Control that they had negotiated the Pass and were now over the Chilean town of Curico. He was told to turn right and start his descent.

Unfortunately, the plane had been slowed by a headwind and the co-pilot had badly misread his position. Turning right took him straight into the high mountains. When an air pocket dropped the plane out of the clouds, the startled pilot realized his error, but attempts to lift the propeller plane back up were defeated by the thin air. One wing clipped a mountain and broke off, taking the tail section and seven people with it. The other wing followed, and the fuselage dropped on to the mountainside like a ski-jumper, forcing the seats loose of their mountings and slamming them forward. It careened toboggan-style down the slope, and finally came to rest in the deep snow. Ill luck and the co-pilot's poor judgement had left them in one of the planet's least accessible places.

There were, for the moment, thirty-three survivors. Seven had had been sucked out with the tail section, four crushed in the cabin; the pilot at his controls. The severely wounded co-pilot could not be extricated from his seat and died during the first night. Four more passengers suffered the same fate, succumbing to a combination of injuries, shock and the intense cold. When morning rose on the Fairchild's half-buried fuselage, only twenty-eight of the original forty-five remained alive.

Those unshocked enough to take stock of their situation had little reason for optimism. They were, as they later discovered, 11,500 feet up in the mountains. At this altitude it got extremely cold – minus 30°C on some nights. And all they could see were other snow-covered slopes and sky – there was no hint of life-giving vegetation.

Not knowing their location would have been bad enough, but mistakenly thinking that they did know it proved even worse. During his final hours the co-pilot had deliriously repeated that they had passed

Survival against the odds: arguments about the Eucharist apparently swayed some victims into becoming survivors – by eating human flesh

Curico, and the surviving passengers had no reason to disbelieve him. As a consequence, their early attempts to reach safety on foot would all be based on a false premise. The list of bad luck continued. The radio would receive but not transmit. The plane had a white roof, which made it practically invisible from the air. And last but far from least, they had very little food and drink aboard – some chocolate, a few crackers and some jam, wine and brandy they had bought on their stopover in Mendoza.

There were some reasons for optimism.

The search for their missing plane was surely under way. They had no medicine, but they did have two medical students – Canessa and Zerbino – who had already proved their resourcefulness. The fact that many of them were already part of a team also proved of enormous importance. It was team effort that turned the gaping fuselage into a rough shelter on the very first night, team spirit that kept them going in the weeks and months which followed.

For the first few days they ate minute portions of chocolate, watched the skies and hoped. A couple of planes were sighted, but did not spot them. On the fourth day, having fashioned some rough snowshoes, a small party set out to look for the tail of the plane. This had contained the batteries they needed to make the radio work, perhaps some food. They were even hopeful of finding other survivors. In the event they found nothing, and turned back

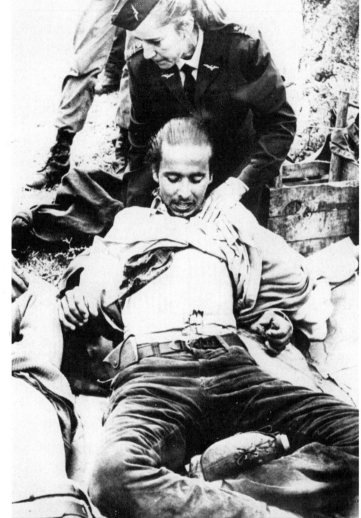

Missing for seventy days: Eating their friends and team-mates was the only way to survive

when their own physical weakness started to scare them.

On the eighth day another passenger, Susana Parrado, died from her injuries. Two days later the remaining survivors discovered from the radio that the official search for their plane had been called off. Chilean, Argentine and Uruguayan search planes had all braved the treacherous mountain winds but found nothing. More than enough snow had fallen to cover the Fairchild, and if anyone had been lucky enough to survive the crash, they could hardly have survived ten days in the mountains. The presumption was death.

Some, at least, of the parents refused to accept it. They paid for searches of their own and consulted the well-known Dutch clairvoyant Gerard Croizet. Whatever the parents' beliefs on such things, he apparently caught a glimpse of the plane's fate, giving them some hope. He actually

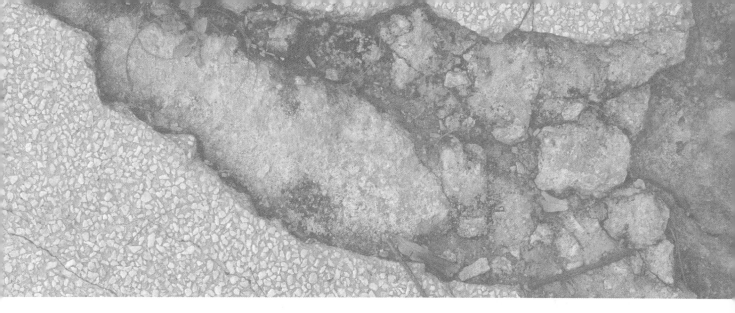

got several of the circumstances right, but the plane's location was not one of them, and searches flown to his specifications came up empty.

High in the mountains, a decision loomed. The possibility of cannibalism had occurred to several survivors, and had occasionally been broached under the cover of black humour. Now, with the food gone and no obvious hope of rescue, it had become a matter of cannibalism or death. Canessa led the argument. Their only hope, he said, was for some of them to walk out of the mountains, and there was no chance of their finding the strength to do that without food. Because soon they would be so weak that they wouldn't have the strength to cut up the bodies in the snow.

Canessa used religion to reinforce his argument. It was just meat, he said. The souls of the dead were now in heaven. The survivors had a duty to keep themselves alive, and the corporeal remains of their friends were their only means of doing so. When someone asked what their dead friends would have thought of such an argument, the other medical student

> **As Uruguayans they came from a culture accustomed to meat in the raw, and lots of it.**

Zerbino had an answer. If his dead body could help his friends stay alive, then he hoped they would make use of it. If they didn't, he said, he would come back and give them a good kicking.

This argument convinced some, but not all. The discussion continued into the afternoon, finally fading into a silence of indecision.

There were two other factors which would make the idea of cannibalism easier to deal with. As Uruguayans they came from a culture still accustomed to meat in the raw, and lots of it. And as Catholics they found themselves with a couple of ready-made justifications for eating the dead – the example of the Eucharist and the duty to preserve life if at all possible.

Eventually Canessa, Zerbino and two others got up and went outside. Canessa took a shard of glass, cut several strips of flesh from a half-covered body and laid them out on the fuselage roof. Back inside he told the gathering that the strips were there, drying in the sun, and that those who wanted them should take them. No one moved, whereupon Canessa went back outside and took one himself. After a brief hesitation, he placed it in his mouth and swallowed.

Most of the others followed his example with varying degrees of acceptance. Others were persuaded by Algorta's announcement, after eating a piece of human flesh, that it was 'like the Holy Communion. When Christ died he gave his body to us so that we can have spiritual life. My friend has given us this body so that we can have physical life' (see Read, Bibliography). Soon only the two oldest survivors – Liliana and Javier Methol – were holding out. They eventually decided that they owed it to their children to survive.

Some of the survivors adapted to their new diet without too much difficulty once the taboo had been broken, while others never got used to the idea. Some used cooking – and some of the precious fuel – to get them past the first hurdle, and then managed to eat the meat raw. Others refused at first to eat it at all, but eventually succumbed. Even then, they were only prepared to eat the fat. The pioneers, spurred on by Canessa's knowledge of nutrition, graduated to organs like the heart and liver.

Another week went by. They were alive and eating, but their human larder was not infinite, and there was no prospect of rescue. The unofficial leaders of the group started planning their own rescue

> **A press conference was called and one survivor, Delgado, outlined the 'communion defence'...the example of the Last Supper had inspired them.**

expedition, but disaster struck before they could implement it. Two avalanches hit the plane in a matter of hours, the first burying eight people alive, the second virtually burying the plane. The eighteen survivors burrowed themselves out and started again.

On 17 November, more than a month after the crash, three of the young men – Canessa, Parrado (brother of the girl who had died) and Vizintin – started down the mountain. Thanks to the co-pilot's mistake over Curico, they were walking in completely the wrong direction, deeper into the mountains. It took them two days to realize this, and more to regain the plane. Another man had died in their absence.

After the failure of this expedition, and the physical exhaustion it had engendered, thoughts turned to repairing the radio, which meant extracting it from the cockpit, taking it down the mountain to the battery, and somehow rewiring it. The effort consumed several days, but ended in vain. Another expedition was decided on, this time in the opposite direction. On 17 December the same three started up the mountain, hoping for a view of Chile from the top. They soon realized that the journey would take longer than expected, and Vizintin was sent back to conserve supplies. Canessa and Parrado continued to climb, each ridge looking like the last, and each ridge stretching seemingly to

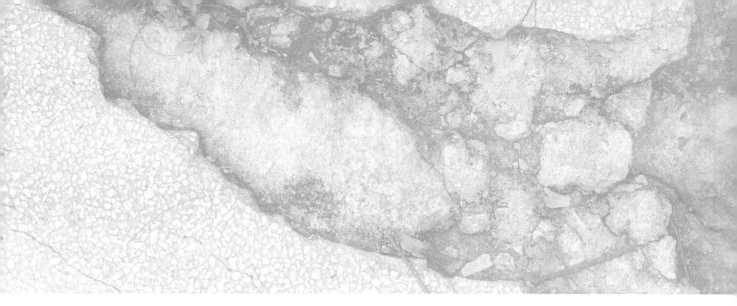

infinity. Four days after setting out they reached the end of the snow. Grass and flowers covered the ground. Birds flew in the sky. By this time Canessa could hardly walk, but they knew they had made it.

Next day they ran into a poor Chilean peasant, who gave them a little bread and went to collect a local farmer. He took them to his farm, fed them, and invited them to take a siesta. It was the afternoon of 21 December. They had been missing for seventy days.

The local authorities arrived; a rescue mission swung into action. Parrado guided a Chilean helicopter back up the mountain to the stricken plane, where the other sixteen had already heard the good news on the radio. Over the next day or so, they were transported down to a local hospital. The reason for their survival was already seeping out – some had admitted their cannibalism to their rescuers, others to a local priest at the hospital. They made no attempt to hide it from the doctors who tended them, who wanted to know how they had survived. In Santiago, a Uruguayan Jesuit who taught at a local college was invited to talk to the survivors,

Soon only...Liliana and Javier Methol were holding out. They eventually decided that they owed it to their children to survive.

and heard their story. He readily agreed that they had done the right thing, and was impressed by their use of the communion parallel for inspiration.

In public, however, the survivors continued to deny the increasingly insistent rumours that swirled around them. It was only once they got back to Montevideo that they realized – or finally accepted – that denial was no longer an option. A press conference was called and one survivor, Delgado, outlined the 'communion defence'.

When they had reached the end of their food, he told the assembled press, the example of Jesus and his Last Supper had inspired them. If Jesus could share his body with his disciples, then they could do the same for each other.

Some of the Andes survivors convinced themselves that this was true, but most saw the 'communion defence' as little more than compassionate public relations, a spin on events which exculpated them, while simultaneously sparing the feelings of those whose relatives and friends had died and been eaten.

4: Famine And Cannibalism

Famine

The last few pages have been concerned with what might be called localized shortages of food. These were caused by human mistakes of one sort or another, and only affected a relative few, but many of the famines which have stalked the earth since the birth of agriculture 8,000 years ago, have had more natural causes.

During these famines, whole populations have had nothing to eat but each other. Unfortunately, their lot was usually common to their fellow countrymen, and hardly newsworthy. Moreover, those who died and those who ate them were almost always poor, usually illiterate, and, more often than not, disinclined to admit, in writing or otherwise, to their new diet. As a result, the recorded instances of famine-induced cannibalism are few and far between. Common sense suggests that it must have taken place on the widest scale, and there is enough recorded evidence to confirm that suggestion, but the real proof is thin on the ground. This is one crime where you really can eat the evidence.

That said, there are stories of parents eating their children in the Italian famine of AD 450, and of the English and Irish doing much the same at the end of the seventh century. It was the turn of the Germans and Bulgarians in circa AD 850, and the Scots were busy devouring each other in AD 936. Twenty serious famines are recorded between the mid-ninth and tenth centuries in northern Europe, each lasting three or four years, and the final decades of the tenth century saw hunger grip most of Europe. According to one nineteenth-century French historian, this terrible famine 'forced people to dine not only on foul animals and reptiles, but also on the flesh of living people, men, women and children. Their need was so great that they even ate their parents. In fact, so severe was the famine that young men ate their mothers and, forgetting all maternal instincts, mothers ate their little ones' (see Tannahill, Bibliography).

The other great civilizations of the world, lying, as they did, in less temperate latitudes, were even more prone to famine. Indian literature and government records are mostly silent on the matter, but some old stories let the cat out of the bag. One from *The Tales of the Ten Princes* tells of a drought lasting twelve years, and the famine that accompanied it. In one household three brothers ate their grain and then, one by one, 'their goats, their sheep, their buffaloes, their cows, their

...the terrible famine, 'forced people to dine not only on foul animals and reptiles, but also on the flesh of living people, men, women and children.'

maidservants, their menservants, their children, and the wives of the eldest and middle brother.' At which point the youngest brother, who 'could not bring himself to eat his darling', grabbed her hand and ran for it (see Tannahill, Bibliography).

The great Egyptian famine

One famous account of a famine, and the horrors to which such deprivation could lead, concerned the great Egyptian famine of 1200–1201. Abd al-Latif, a doctor in his thirties, had only just arrived from Baghdad when the tragedy began to unfold. Egypt's farmers relied on the annual Nile floods to revitalize their soil, but the waters failed in 1200, drought took hold, and thousands fled to the imaginary refuge of cities like Misr and Cairo. In the spring of 1201, 'the air became corrupt, and pestilence and a deadly contagion began to take their toll, and the poor,

under the pressure of ever-growing want, ate carrion, corpses, dogs, excrement and animal dung. They went further and reached the stage of eating little children' (see al-Latif, Bibliography).

Al-Latif witnessed many such incidents, and the punishment of those responsible. 'I myself saw a little roast child in a basket. It was brought to the commandant, and led in at the same time were a man and a woman who were the child's father and mother. The commandant condemned them to be burned alive' (see al-Latif, Bibliography). Al-Latif noticed that in the early stages of the famine, no one could stop talking about the increasing incidences of cannibalism. But soon people got used to the idea, and even fond of human flesh. Stocks were laid in and new recipes devised. 'The horror people had felt at first vanished entirely; one spoke of it, and heard it spoken of, as a matter of everyday indifference' (see al-Latif, Bibliography).

Unlike those tribes who would eat anyone but their own relatives, the citizens of thirteenth-century Egypt seemed keen to keep things in the family, or at least pretend that that was what they were doing. The corpse they were eating was always the corpse of a husband, son or

Saving energy by sleeping, May 1946: during the post-war years, China suffered a bad famine during which incidents of cannibalism were documented

other close relative. Far better, they claimed, that they should eat their own family than see them consumed by strangers.

As usual, the cannibalism had begun with the eating of the dead, then moved on to murder for the purposes of consumption. Babies were attacked in their mother's arms, children taken from the streets. Those cannibals who were caught supplied their own fair share of food – 'When some unfortunate who had been convicted of eating flesh was burned alive, the corpse was always found to have been devoured by the following morning. People ate it the more willingly, for the flesh, being fully roasted, was in no need of cooking' (see al-Latif, Bibliography).

Chinese famines

The Chinese were much more detailed when it came to keeping records. Imperial documents list 131 famines – most of them caused by drought – between the beginning of the Han Dynasty in 221 BC and the end of the Ming Dynasty in AD 1644. In one of the earliest, half the population died, and Emperor Kao Tzu allowed his grateful subjects to eat or sell their children. A famous novel written at the end of the Ming Dynasty – His Yu Chi's *A Journey to the West* – was full of descriptions of cannibalism, and contained some useful advice. This advice consisted of the belief that the eating of only two kinds of human flesh was guaranteed to prolong the consumer's life – the flesh of a young child (especially the heart and liver) and that of a Tibetan Buddhist monk who had attained Buddhahood through his own efforts over ten generations. The latter was probably harder to find.

In more recent times, over-population increased the frequency and severity of Chinese famines, and the cannibalism which they provoked. The famine of 1874-7 was particularly serious. The Roman Catholic Bishop of Shansi reported in 1877 that husbands were eating their wives, parents eating their sons and daughters, children eating their parents. Thirty years later, famine hit the province of Shensi. In the capital Xian human flesh was soon on sale. A new kind of meatball appeared, made from the bodies of the dead. It sold for around four American cents per pound, and soon became a staple of the local diet.

Famine in war

Many famines have had natural causes – drought, insect infestations, hailstones, flood, blighted crops – but many others have been caused, wilfully or not, by human action. One of the surest routes to famine over the centuries has been the waging of war. In the days before General Issue rations, armies used to work their way across country like locusts, consuming whatever was available and leaving the unlucky inhabitants with only what they had managed to hide – the nice armies, that was. The nasty ones implemented 'scorched earth' policies as well, which were intended to render the land unfit for future cultivation.

Sieges played a prominent role in wars right up the Second World War – Leningrad and Stalingrad being two of the prime examples discussed below. The idea was usually to blockade a castle or town until the food inside ran out, weakening the defenders and forcing them to surrender, which frequently happened. Occasionally though the biter got bit, and the besiegers' food supplies ran out first.

Prisoners are another group who have often been at risk, either from their own hunger or that of their jailers. The degree of intent in such circumstances can vary widely. When Rudolf Höss, the Nazi Commandant of Auschwitz noticed that his Russian prisoners were eating each other, he put it down to their no longer being human beings. Höss would appear to have had a somewhat stunted awareness of humanity – the reason for the Russians eating each other was the German failure to give them any other kind of sustenance.

There are countless recorded instances of cannibalism in war, some more believable than others. Julius Caesar noted the practice during the siege of Alesia in Gaul, but, like most soldiers and statesmen down the centuries, had a vested interest in making the enemy look bad. We can be a little more certain about the tales of cannibalism in Paris during the siege of 1871, but the story of a butcher's shop on St Louis selling human flesh sounds a shade apocryphal. Much more recently there have been tales of cannibalism in Rwanda during the genocide of 1994 and Bosnia-Herzegovina during the civil wars which accompanied the break-up of Yugoslavia. Despite the apparent ubiquity of today's media it remains impossible to say for certain what such tales represent – simple truth or the endless inventiveness of hostile propagandists.

Late in the Han period one general famously killed his most beloved concubine to feed his starving soldiers.

China

There are many recorded instances in Chinese history of war-related famine.

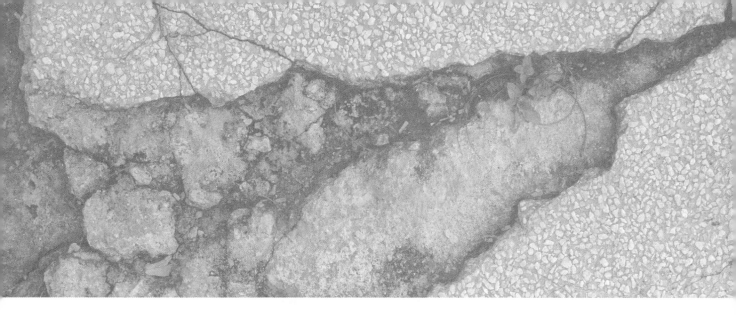

During the siege of the Sung capital in 594 BC, an envoy from the Sung monarch told the besiegers that he had been sent to tell them how bad things were. In the city families were 'exchanging' their children, he said, and using the bones for the fuel. The idea of 'exchanging' children would recur with some frequency in Chinese history, and put them – as far as war was concerned – firmly in the camp of those who thought it better to eat the children of others than one's own.

Many other sieges ended in the same predicament. In Chao, the exchange of children was followed by a slaughter of the concubines to feed the defending soldiers. Concubines had a particularly raw deal in China. Late in the Han period one general famously killed his most beloved concubine to feed his starving soldiers. Touched by this self-sacrifice – the general's, not the concubine's – the newly-fed soldiers fought to the death. The trick worked so well that it was repeated at least once, much to another concubine's despair. She was turned into soup for the brave soldiers.

The most dramatic of sieges took place in Honan during the T'ang period. The besieged men of Sui-yang ate their horses, their old, their children, their women and eventually themselves. When the town finally fell, only 4,000 of 60,000 inhabitants remained. Their fate is unrecorded.

Crusaders and Saracens

Europe and the Middle East also had their share of grisly sieges, and the most grisly of all concerned one of the former's perennial attempts to control the latter. The Crusades were noted for their barbarism – particularly on the Christian side – and eating the enemy out of spite was one habit of which both sides were occasionally guilty. Famine-generated cannibalism seems to have mostly occurred during Crusader sieges of Muslim towns and castles.

The besiegers of Antioch in 1098 had their own cannibal detachment, the Tarfurs. This band of beggar vagabonds had attached themselves to the First Crusade and adopted a de-horsed Norman nobleman as their leader. When food ran short outside Antioch, the Crusader leader Peter the Hermit suggested that the Tarfurs ease their hunger by roasting and eating some of the Muslim dead that were scattered around the camp. Having done so, and enjoying the effect that this had on the living enemy inside Antioch – who now 'feared death from the lances of the knights less than the further

The religious differences between the combatants in the Crusades meant that stories of cannibalism – and the non-respect of the enemy therein – were legion

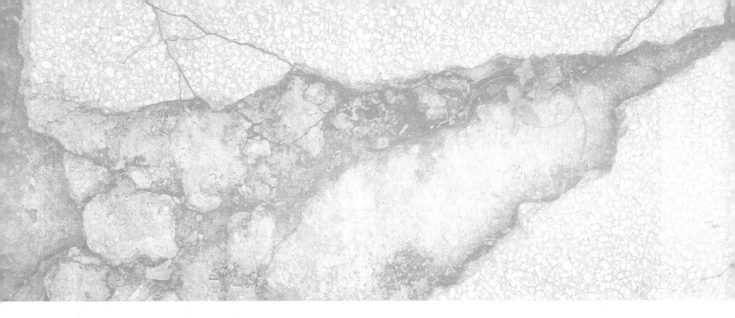

When food ran short outside Antioch, the Crusader leader, Peter the Hermit, suggested that the Tarfurs ease their hunger by roasting and eating some of the Muslim dead that were scattered around the camp.

consummation they heard of, under the teeth of the Tarfurs' (see Tannahill, Bibliography) – the last-named took to desecrating cemeteries and digging up Muslim corpses for consumption.

Worse happened during the siege of Ma'arrat later that year. 'I shudder to say that many of our men, terribly tormented by the madness of starvation, cut pieces of flesh from the buttocks of the Saracens lying there dead. These pieces they cooked and ate, savagely devouring the flesh while it was insufficiently roasted. In this way, the besiegers were more harmed than the besieged' (see Price, Bibliography). A moot point, one would think. Other reports had adults boiled in pots and impaled children grilled on spits over open fires. Much the same happened during the frenzy that followed the taking of Jerusalem in the following year.

A century later, during the Third Crusade, Richard the Lionheart was said to have eaten curried Saracen. Some accounts stress that he believed the meat to be pork, but all accounts agree that – once apprised of what he had just eaten – he used the fact to cause consternation among the Saracen ambassadors he was engaged in receiving.

The Mongols

The Mongol armies which swept across Eurasia in the thirteenth century were not social democrats. When it came to savagery they had few peers, and few of their military leaders were ever prepared to let their already precarious sense of common humanity overrule what seemed expedient. They did not leave mountains of skulls where cities had been because they looked pretty – they did it to disencourage *les autres*. And when they offered a besieged city the choice between surrender or death, they meant it. It would not do for the next city to harbour any false hopes.

Whether they indulged in cannibalism is open to doubt. No serious famine seems to have befallen their empire in the brief century or so of its existence, and even if one had, it seems unlikely that the Mongols themselves would have gone hungry. They certainly drank the blood of their horses when no other sustenance was available, but accounts of Crusader-style behaviour are rare.

One such was presented by Matthew Paris in his thirteenth-century book, *Chronica Major*. 'The Tartar [Mongol] chiefs, with the houndish cannibals their followers, fed upon the flesh of their carcasses as if they had been bread, and left nothing but bones for the vultures. But, wonderful to tell, the vultures, hungry and ravenous, would not condescend to eat the remnants of flesh, if any by chance were left. The old and ugly women were given to their dog-headed cannibals – anthrophags as they are called – to be their daily food; but those who were beautiful were saved alive, to be stifled and overwhelmed by the number of their ravishers, in spite of all their cries and lamentations. Virgins were deflowered until they died of exhaustion; then, their breasts were cut off to be kept as dainties for their chiefs, and their bodies furnished a jovial banquet to the savages' (see Price, Bibliography).

It seems no coincidence that this was written in 1243, two years after the Mongol armies panicked Europe by reaching the Adriatic and central Poland. It reads like propaganda and almost certainly was.

There are other stories. One had Abaga, a grandson of Genghis Khan and the Mongol ruler of Persia in the late thirteenth century, demanding that a

Mongol conqueror Genghis Khan: stories of cannibalism in Tartar culture were almost certainly fabrications

Turkish traitor be cut up and regularly added to his normal meals. Another had the same unlucky Turk boiled, minced and served up to the army as an example to others. At various times the Mongols were said to be overfond of succulent young girls, and accused of eating everyone. Tannahill, in her excellent history of the cannibal complex, points out that 'as nomadic herdsmen, the Mongols seldom if ever suffered from meat shortages', and, 'like most armies in history, knew far better uses for women than serving them up in a stew' (see Tannahill, Bibliography).

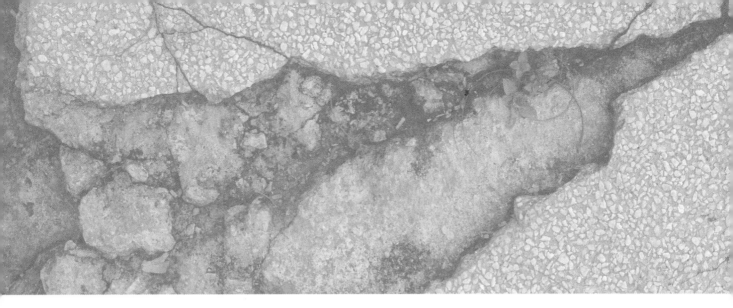

1812

When Napoleon Bonaparte launched his invasion of Russia on 24 June 1812 few realized that the Corsican genius had finally bitten off considerably more than he could chew. His 450,000-strong Grande Armee faced much smaller Russian armies led by inexperienced generals, and he fully expected to be receiving the Tsar's cringing surrender before autumn turned to winter.

The Russians, however, refused to co-operate, laying waste the land as they fell back towards distant Moscow. Twice the French had to stop to wait for much-needed supplies, and by August they had only reached Smolensk. Only by reaching Moscow, Napoleon reasoned, could he force the Tsar into accepting defeat.

He marched on into autumn, fighting the bloody and indecisive battle of Borodino some miles outside Moscow. The new Russian commander, Kutuzov, withdrew to the city and kept on withdrawing. When Napoleon entered it on 14 September he found it empty of both food and Tsar. A few days later the city caught fire – whether by accident or design is disputed – and became, if possible, an even less desirable residence. After a few weeks of waiting in vain for some sort of political move or other, Napoleon and his army,

now little more than 100,000 strong, abandoned the city and started retracing their steps. The frost set in the very next day, and by 4 November, the snow was coming down in earnest.

A further battle was fought by the River Beresina on 28–29 November, killing another 25,000 Frenchmen, and turning the Grande Armee's retreat into a long and infinitely painful rout. Napoleon himself headed for Paris, but his soldiers had fewer options. One French nobleman watched his fellow countrymen burn whole houses to get a little warmth, and other delirious soldiers hurl themselves into the conflagrations. 'Their starving companions watched them die without apparent horror. There were even some who laid hold of bodies disfigured and roasted by the flames and – incredible as it seems – ventured to carry this loathsome food to their mouths' (see Askenasy, Bibliography).

This must have been early in the retreat – by December such scenes were all too credible. By then the horses had all been eaten, and cannibalism – first of the dead, and then of the living – had become commonplace. Russian witnesses reported that 'they had often met Frenchmen in some barn, sitting round a fire on the

Peasants took to using their barns and stables as freezers, stacking the human dead for future consumption.

bodies of their dead comrades, from whom they had cut the best parts to satisfy their hunger. Later, they grew weaker and weaker, and fell dead only to be eaten in turn by other comrades' (see Tannahill, Bibliography). Of the 450,000 men who crossed the Niemen in June, a mere 20,000 returned.

Russian civil war

Famine convulsed some of the same areas in the early 1920s, but this time it was Russians and Ukrainians who suffered. There had been serious food shortages during the years of Russia's involvement in the First World War, and as the 1917 Revolution mutated into civil war they grew more acute. The troops sent into the countryside to gather food for the cities paid little heed to the needs of the countryside. Bad harvests in 1920 and 1921 made things even worse, and by the summer of the second year a vast area of the southern steppe – stretching from eastern Ukraine to the Ural Mountains – was running desperately short of anything to eat. People began dying in droves.

The Russian – now Soviet – people had been at war for seven, long, brutalizing years. They had become accustomed to bloodshed, and life – both others' and their own – had become devalued. The psychiatrist Petr Gannushkin told the Soviet leader Lenin that half the population was now suffering from some kind of mental illness. It was not normal, he was reported to have told the Soviet leader, for sons to kill their fathers and fathers their sons.

In the famine region, many normal restraints had already reached breaking point. Government officials or soldiers caught by the outraged peasants were treated with great cruelty – flayed, disembowelled, and tied to trees by their own intestines. In such times the human body was flesh and blood, and nothing more.

That summer and autumn the peasants of the steppes ate their cats, their dogs and any vermin they could catch. They ate grass and tree bark. By November, when the snows came to cover the last vestiges of edible vegetation, there was nothing left. 'There has been no grain in the village since Easter,' one peasant wrote. 'Yesterday, I stumbled on the body of a young boy, no more than six or seven years old. I took it home, carved off the flesh and began to eat. It was the best meal I'd had all year' (see Figes, Bibliography).

He was not alone. Thousands of cases of cannibalism were reported over the next few months, and thousands more went unrecorded. Mothers, desperate to feed their children, cut the limbs off corpses and boiled the flesh in pots. In the beginning, people seem to have stuck to eating their dead relatives. The youngest children, many of whom had been early victims of the famine, were valued for their sweeter taste. Peasants took to using

Cannibalism in such desperate circumstances as those depicted here cannot be condemned as harshly as purely criminal acts such as desire cannibalism. Refugees from the Russian Civil War were often forced to live in the woods – and many were glad for that

their barns and stables as freezers, stacking the dead for future consumption.

At first there seems to have been some – understandable – reluctance to admit what was going on. 'There are several cafeterias in our village, and all of them serve up young children,' one man said. 'Everyone eats human flesh, but they hide it' (see Figes, Bibliography). Desperation soon overcame such scruples. 'We will not give him up,' one woman caught feeding her dead husband to her son, told police. 'We need him for food, he is our own family, and no one has the right to take him away from us' (see Figes, Bibliography). Others defended the practice on philosophical grounds. The souls had already departed the bodies, they said, so why should the worms get the food?

The Russians have a word for this: *trupoyedstvo* – the eating of flesh from a corpse. This type of cannibalism was

A woman pulls a corpse on a sledge down Leningrad's main avenue, 1942. Many died of starvation during the siege of Leningrad

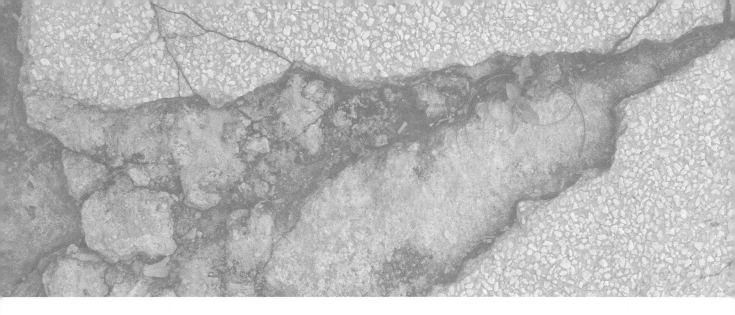

'We will not give him up,' one woman caught feeding her dead husband to her son, told police.

understandable, even morally acceptable, in such desperate circumstances. They had a different word – *lyudoyedstvo* – for the killing and eating of a fellow human. This type of cannibalism was considered unacceptable in any circumstances, but during the famine it went on regardless.

Some of this killing was done with a meal in mind – there were gangs of hungry adults who targeted children, gangs of hungry children who targeted adults. But many murders were for profit. In times of famine meat prices go up, and people are less inclined to ask where a particular steak or chop comes from. Visiting the home of one Ukrainian couple who sold rissoles in the local town, police and medical inspectors discovered barrels of children's bodyparts, sorted and salted. One of the inspectors felt somewhat queasy – he had eaten one of the couple's rissoles for lunch.

During these years many of his fellow citizens had unknowingly eaten similar fare. Those officials charged with finding enough food to feed the cities were not inclined to question a good supplier of meat, and many victims of the famine were recycled in the local cafeterias and factory canteens of the new Soviet state.

The siege of Leningrad

On 22 June 1941, Hitler launched Operation Barbarossa, the invasion of the Soviet Union. Thanks to Mussolini's bungling attack on Greece, and the subsequent need for German help, the invasion began several weeks later than planned. The German generals who knew their military history – and that was most of them – duly noted that they were only two days ahead of Napoleon. Tanks might eat up the miles, but most of the German Army still travelled by foot or horse.

The attack was launched in three directions, towards Kiev in the south, Moscow in the centre and Leningrad (now St Petersburg) in the north. Kiev was taken by mid-September. German troops reached the suburbs of Moscow in early December, but were then thrown back. Leningrad was completely surrounded by the Germans and their Finnish allies on 15 September. Around three million people were trapped, and those who survived would remain so for 900 days.

After the war, the police, military and medical records kept during the siege were censored to remove any possible stains on the city's character. Leningrad was a 'Hero City', and the new Museum of the Siege was organized accordingly. There was no mention of the terrible things that people had done to each other in the struggle to survive. No mention, in particular, of the widespread cannibalism which had taken place. It was only with the end of communism, and the opening up of the old records, that a fuller, more truthful story came to light.

By December 1941, most Leningraders lived in fear of the cannibals.

The first winter was the worst. Thousands were killed or wounded by artillery bombardment, but nature and shortages killed far more – over half a million people in four months. Hitler, like Napoleon, had unwittingly picked one of the coldest winters on record for his fatal adventure, and his denim-clad soldiers suffered accordingly. They, however, had food to eat. The people of Leningrad, and the Soviet soldiers defending them, were running short of this precious commodity from the moment the siege took hold. They also lacked any public heating, light or water. Once the nearby Lake Ladoga was frozen, some supplies could be brought in on the 'ice road', but nowhere near enough to feed three million people.

Once normal food became scarce, people took to eating what they could. The birds had already left the city, those that had not frozen to death in mid-flight and dropped out of the sky. Pet dogs and cats were eventually consumed, often with great reluctance by their owners. One man tried to hang himself after eating his cat, but the rope broke. He broke his leg in the fall, and froze to death.

Grass and plants were torn from the freezing ground, bark stripped from trees, carpenters' glue melted down and ironically dubbed 'meat in aspic'. Thousands were dying each day, and desperation was growing. The number of people attacked and killed for food – or, more usually, their monthly ration card – escalated sharply. Notices of missing children started appearing in windows and on boards at street corners. They might have been killed by a stray shell, or simply dropped dead from the hunger and cold. Or had they fallen prey to something worse? As early as October the dark rumours of cannibalism began to circulate.

Who could be surprised? At the city's main outdoor market – the Haymarket – bread had taken over from money as the main currency. Vodka came in a good second. Money, though, could still buy you some 'Badayev earth'. A sugar plant in the city had burned down, and the earth beneath it had become saturated with molten sugar. The top three feet of earth fetched 100 roubles a glass, the deeper deposits somewhat less.

And soon there some were suspicious-looking meat patties on sale. People tried

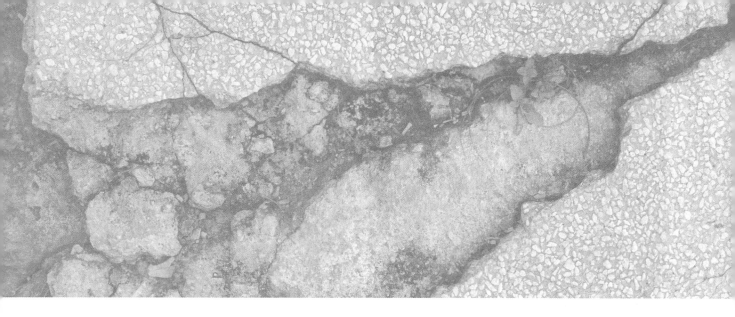

to convince themselves that these strange-tasting confections were made of horse, dog, cat or rat, but the delusion got harder and harder to sustain. The evidence of cannibalism was becoming impossible to ignore. With the cemeteries overflowing, many corpses were left in the snow where they fell, refrigerated meat for whoever needed it most. People would pass the same corpse each day, noting the new cuts which had been made under cover of darkness. One walker in the night came across three heads lying in a snowdrift, those of a man, a woman, and a small girl with plaited blonde hair. Cannibalism was the only explanation he could think of.

Those in the cemeteries were far from safe. Coffins would be opened to reveal a head and two feet – the rest had been carried away. One woman, stopped while leaving a cemetery, was found to have the bodies of five children stacked on her toboggan.

It was not just the dead being eaten, either. One young couple went to barter for some boots at the Haymarket. The seller had only brought one boot with him, and offered to take the young man back to his flat to get the other. As they reached their destination the young man, Dmitri, started wondering why his companion

looked so well fed. He soon found out. The seller knocked on a door and told someone inside: 'It is me, with a live one.' Dmitri had a whiff of something strange, a glimpse of white meat hanging on hooks, and ran. As fortune would have it, a small army truck was passing by. 'Cannibals!' he shouted, pointing behind him. The soldiers poured in, shots rang out. They had indeed been human torsos on the hooks.

Dmitri was luckier than many. By December 1941, most Leningraders lived in fear of the cannibals. Many guessed who they were – in an ocean of emaciated ghosts these men with soft, fat faces and

Hitler, like Napoleon, had unwittingly picked one of the coldest winters for his fatal adventure.

over-bright eyes stuck out like sore thumbs – but few could prove it. Rumours abounded of cannibal organizations, Mason-like fraternities who met for special feasts. Cuts from corpses were not good enough for them – they insisted on freshly-killed meat, and sent their killers out to get it. Ordinary Leningraders tried to keep their children at home, and tried to avoid the unlit streets in the long hours of darkness, but it was not always possible.

Perhaps the most surprising thing about the Leningrad siege was the strength of the official determination to stamp out cannibalism in what was, by any definition, a starving city. From the beginning of the siege, anyone found with a stolen ration card or illicit food was likely to be shot on the spot, and anyone found cutting up corpses was likely to suffer the same fate. By mid-February 1942, over 900 people had been arrested for cannibalism, and by the middle of that year around 1,000 a month were being taken into custody. NKVD (the People's Commissariat of Internal Affairs) records show that at least 600 of them were executed. The police also used the darker rumours to scare their criminal and political suspects into confession. If they refused, they would be thrown into the cannibals' cell, 'where they ate each other' (see Salisbury, Bibliography).

The siege of Stalingrad

The other great siege of the Second World War was of Stalingrad (now Volgograd). Though of greater military significance, these lasted only a few terrible months. In September 1942, the Nazi armies enveloped the city on three sides, forcing the Soviets to supply it across the fourth, the two-mile wide River Volga. In late November, two converging Soviet armies cut across the Germans' rear and joined hands, creating a siege of their own. This was brought to an end by a two-stage surrender of the German forces inside the

city, on 31 January and 2 February 1943.

There were instances of cannibalism, but they were few and far between when compared to Leningrad. Most of the civilian population was evacuated before the battle got going, and food supplies, though far from generous, continued to reach the Soviet soldiers and workers' militias in the increasingly derelict city. Only one group of people were starving,

September 1942: women, children and old men cluster on the outskirts of Stalingrad, forced there by the Nazis' shelling

and their condition was hardly a consequence of war. With the same savage disregard for the laws of war which they had shown throughout the campaign, the Germans neglected to feed their Russian prisoners. Many of those who died were eaten by their starving comrades.

After their surrender, it was the Germans' turn. The 90,000 Wehrmacht soldiers who

...Leningraders tried to keep their children at home, tried to avoid the unlit streets...

remained of the original force of 250,000 were loaded onto trains for prison camps in the distant interior, frequently with inadequate food, sometimes with none for days on end. At the end of journeys, which often took weeks, many prisoners had died in fights for the morsels thrown into the wagons, and few of them had remained unhurt in these fights. The Russians were equally parsimonious with their food in the camps, and cannibalism reportedly flourished to the extent that 'anti-cannibalism teams' were recruited from among the German officers.

There were sundry reports of cannibalism in China and the Pacific, with captured Japanese soldiers usually providing the meal. There were, however, no indications that the consumers were driven by extreme hunger. Anger seemed the most likely bet in China, a habit of revenge in the islands of Melanesia.

The only other places where starvation loomed were the labour and concentration camps which the Nazis spread like a stain across Europe. There were harrowing, isolated reports of individual incidents in many camps, but it was in the final days of the war that the practice grew widespread. Knowing that defeat was imminent, many camp authorities simply abandoned their posts, issuing orders that the prisoners were to remain locked up, and leaving them, in effect, to starve. Lord Russell of Liverpool, visiting Bergen-Belsen after its liberation, heard that one in ten of the high-piled bodies 'had a piece cut from the thigh or other part of the body, which had been taken and eaten.' The same witness told him that on a visit to the mortuary 'I saw a prisoner whip out a knife, cut a portion out of the leg of a dead body and put it quickly in his mouth, naturally

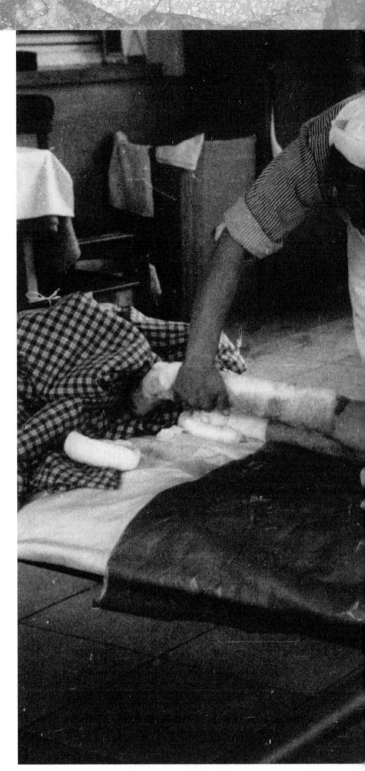

frightened of being seen in the act of doing so. I leave it to your imagination to realize to what state the prisoners were reduced, for men to risk eating bits of flesh cut from corpses' (see Marriner, Bibliography).

There have been many wars since the Second World War, but few of these have

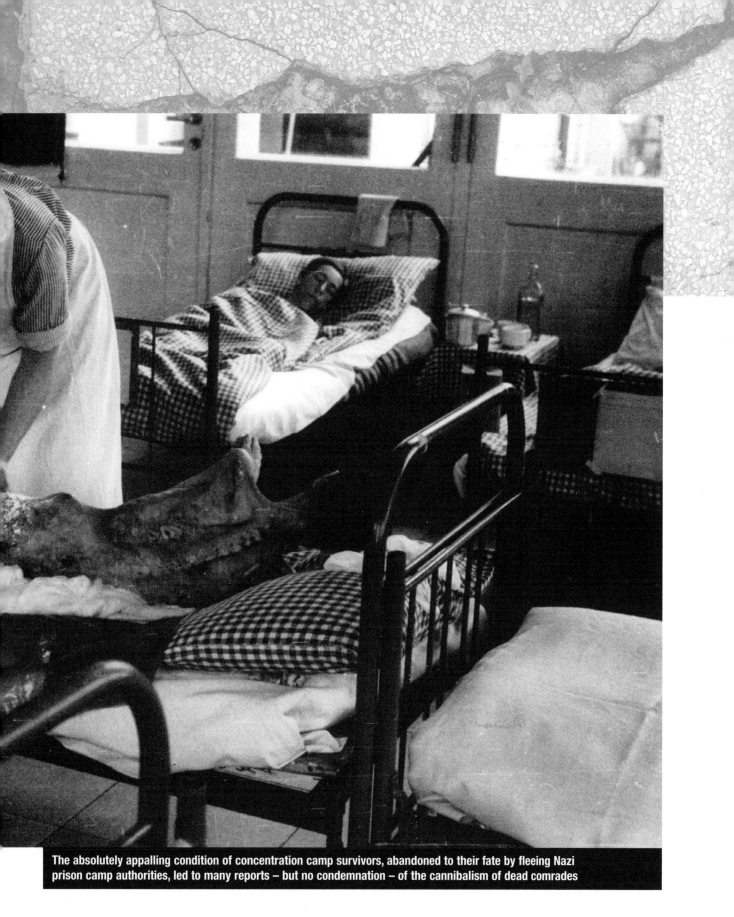

The absolutely appalling condition of concentration camp survivors, abandoned to their fate by fleeing Nazi prison camp authorities, led to many reports – but no condemnation – of the cannibalism of dead comrades

created famine conditions – in Europe, at least. The standard excuse for cannibalism in time of conflict has all but vanished, but fighters continue to feed on each other. Rituals drawn from tribal memory are dusted down, given a polish, and taught to children. And, when all is said and done, there are few more effective weapons of terror than the public eating of one's enemies.

Famines to order

The two great famines of the twentieth century were not caused by war – or not, that is, by war as it is usually understood. No doubt Stalin and Mao Tse-tung, the two men almost wholly responsible for these two famines, would have argued that they were engaged in class wars. But neither was facing any physical threat from their supposed enemies. These two famines were the consequence of ideological and personal ambitions run riot, and a brutal disregard for the lives of ordinary people.

The Soviet collectivization of agriculture

Stalin and his lackeys took the decision to collectivize Soviet agriculture in 1929. Over the following four tempestuous years, all private farms were taken into state ownership. Their owners and farmhands became workers in the new giant collective farms, collecting – when they were lucky – wages like any industrial workers.

The regime had three aims in mind. First and foremost, it had realized that industrializing the Soviet Union required capital. It was not going to come from abroad, and the middle class had been all but wiped out. Creating a new one would take time that Stalin did not think he had. The only alternative was forcing the peasants off their land and into the factories. This would also fulfil the second aim – the neutering of the peasants, and particularly the rich peasants or kulaks, as a potential source of political opposition. Collectivization was intended to break their spirit. The third aim, that of creating a more modern, industrialized agriculture, was almost incidental.

Hardly surprisingly, there was resistance. The peasants hid their tools, hid their grain. The regime dispatched its enforcers. The rich peasants – and anyone who resisted was, by definition, a rich peasant – were either killed or deported to the country's harsher regions. What grain was found was sent to the cities. Food was even taken from tables in mid-meal. The peasants responded by eating their animals, destroying their tools, burning their grain – better that, than let the commissars have them.

Famine settled on the land, particularly in the Ukraine. People were eating straw and nettles, making soup out of tree bark, cooking mice stew. And they were the lucky ones. The regime knew full well what was happening, but the requisitions continued, the storehouses full of grain remained locked and heavily guarded.

Cats and dogs went next, then dead horses. And when all the animals had gone, and the people had started to die in their thousands, the spectre of

> **People were eating straw and nettles, making soup out of tree bark [and] cooking mice stew. The regime knew full well what was happening, but the requisitions continued...**

The 'collectivization' of Russia's peasantry in the early 1930s led to appalling poverty and famine

As in the Soviet Union, people ate what they could find, and this, eventually, included children and the bodies of the dead. Some were caught and shot by the regime, but most were not.

cannibalism re-emerged from its ten-year slumber and, once again, began to stalk the steppes. There were rumours of families devouring their children, more than rumours of street markets dealing in human flesh. Children were kept indoors.

Millions died anyway. Official sources claimed 4.5 million; author Robert Conquest (see Bibliography) puts the combined figure for collectivization and the famine it caused at 13.5 million. No one will ever know for sure. When the Soviet population census of 1937 came up with a larger-than-expected deficit of people, Stalin had the census-takers taken out and shot.

Collectivizing agriculture might have had its merits, but collectivizing it by force had none. Stalin was, however, unmoved by the human cost of collectivization. Half a century later, Soviet agriculture still had not recovered from the trauma. Millions had died – had, in effect, been killed – for absolutely nothing.

The Chinese 'Great Leap Forward'

You might think that Stalin's lasting blunder would have given Mao Tse-tung pause to ponder when it came to doing something similar. Not so. Nine years into

his revolution, he was getting as impatient as Stalin had been. Things were not improving fast enough, and it had to be someone else's fault. The peasantry sprang easily to mind.

In 1953 Mao had promised industrialization in ten to fifteen years, but soon concluded that less would suffice if only the people could be persuaded to show more communist spirit. In 1958 he rammed his foot down on the accelerator pedal, announcing a 'Great Leap Forward'. China would overtake the capitalist countries before you could say Chiang Kai-shek. An enormous increase in agricultural production would be exported to pay for the technology and machinery which China needed to modernize. Millions of peasant farms would be merged into 26,000 super-efficient collective farms or communes. And in addition to their agricultural pursuits, these communes would produce the steel China needed in thousands of small backyard furnaces.

This was a mad pipe dream from the start, and Mao knew it. There was no enormous increase in agricultural production, but that did not stop the Party from exporting a much higher proportion of what food there was. This reduced the

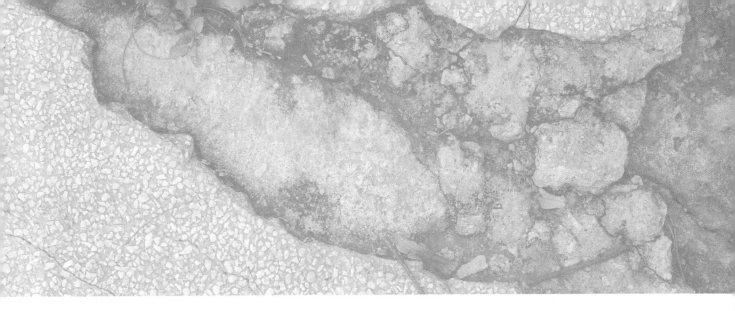

amount available for consumption, and using up huge quantities of grain to make ethyl alcohol missile fuel reduced it still further. Taking peasants away from the land to work the backyard furnaces made things even worse.

As in the Soviet Union, officials ignored peasant pleas that they were being left with nothing to eat. The requisition teams arrived, took what they could find, and left. By the winter of 1958 people were beginning to starve, and over the next two years the situation slowly worsened. People in the cities had an average daily calorie intake lower than that enjoyed by slave labourers in Auschwitz. In the countryside it was far, far less.

Other senior leaders brought this to Mao's attention, but he brushed the protests aside. The 'kind' explanation has Mao believing that the peasants were resisting socialism, and in need of a lesson in revolutionary enthusiasm. The unkind reading has him not giving a damn, has him, in fact, rejoicing in the sheer scale of the sacrifice he had demanded.

China has a long history of famines, but in pre-communist times the usual response was to move outside the famine region in search of food. In 1958–61 the regime

By the winter of 1958 people were beginning to starve, and over the next two years the situation slowly worsened. People in the cities had an average daily calorie intake lower that that enjoyed by slave labourers in Auschwitz. In the countryside it was far, far less.

refused to allow it. As in the Soviet Union, people ate what they could find, and this, eventually, included children and the bodies of the dead. Some were caught and shot by the regime, but most were not. Interviewed decades later, few showed any shame. In China, there were no significant religious or moral taboos against eating human flesh in order to survive.

Mao's was the most devastating famine in history. It killed well over thirty million people. And like Stalin's it served no useful purpose. The backyard steel proved mostly useless, the communes were eventually disbanded, and China's industrial miracle had to wait for the harshest of capitalisms.

Political desperation

Desperation may be an inappropriate word for the last two pieces in this section, but it is hard to see what the appropriate one would be. Both describe widespread acts of cannibalism in circumstances of political frenzy. This cannibalism was neither culturally condoned nor hunger-induced, but in both cases the participants seemed driven by forces beyond their control. Examining their stories, they certainly seemed desperate, but exactly what they were desperate for remains an open question. Cannibalism was not the object of the frenzy, merely one means of expressing it.

The Cultural Revolution in China

Mao Tse-tung launched the Cultural Revolution in 1966, mostly as a means of rooting out enemies and reinforcing his own control of China's destiny. He let a generation of indoctrinated youth loose on the rest of society, armed with a 'Little Red Book' of his own gnomic utterances and instructions to destroy everything that was holding the revolution back. Not surprisingly, the indoctrinated youth adopted a wonderfully inclusive definition of what and who was 'holding the revolution back' – everything and everyone but Mao and themselves.

The official list of class enemies, in the jargon of the day, included traitors, spies, unrepentant capitalists, unreformed landlords, rich peasants, counter-revolutionaries, social dregs and rightists. These were not objective categories, merely labels which could be applied at will by Mao's ardent followers. What this meant in practice was yob culture gone mad. The traditional Chinese respect for tradition, education and the elderly was turned on its head. The past was the enemy, and anything or anyone who represented it – or even looked like they might – was ripe for criticism, 're-education' and, frequently, death. There was no fear of erring on the side of leniency. As one official statement put it – 'wrongly killing a hundred is better than letting one guilty person escape' (see Yi, Bibliography).

In this atmosphere of ideological frenzy, more or less any behaviour was permitted. In later years, people would happily admit to killing their 'enemies'. Chairman Mao had told them – it's us or them, kill or be killed. Many believed it, and many others welcomed the perfect opportunity to settle

Not surprisingly, the indoctrinated youth adopted a wonderfully inclusive definition of what and who was 'holding the revolution back' – everything and everyone but Mao and themselves.

Under the guise of Communism, Mao left millions of his people to be killed by his more ardent followers, and famine

old scores. Threats of accusation were enough to win favours of many kinds, and accusations themselves were almost guaranteed to bring some sort of suffering in their wake.

The victims were numerous. In Binyang County – one small county in southern China – 3,681 people were killed in eleven days during the summer of 1968. For the most part they were beaten or stoned to death. Guns were available, but were officially discouraged. Using clubs, fists and stones would – or so it was thought in high places – make for a more vivid political education. It is not known whether Mao and his cronies considered cannibalising the enemy the height of instructive chic, but it seems a logical progression. Some of their followers certainly thought so.

The full extent of the practice during the Cultural Revolution is unknown, and will remain so as long as Chinese governments revere freedom of expression in much the same way as vampires love sunlight.

However, an intrepid journalist named Zheng Yi did take it upon himself to investigate persistent rumours of cannibalism in the southern province of Guangxi. After escaping both the province and China, he wrote and published an account of his findings, *Scarlet Memorial*.

The stories were many and gruesome. If eating a spy's liver during the civil war was acceptable behaviour, then what could be wrong with consuming the livers of Twenty-three Category types (those earmarked for re-education and/or death during the Cultural Revolution) in 1968? Witnesses remembered a Party official wandering down the street with a human leg over his shoulder, bits of trouser still attached. A school principal was beaten to death, and those responsible tore the flesh from his body before starting a fire.

The levels of cruelty were appallingly high. 'Enemies of the people' were not just killed and then eaten – their livers were cut out and eaten while they were still alive. A heart torn, Aztec-style, from a landlord's son was cut into finger-sized slices, and fought over by a frenzied crowd. Two students were tied up under two big trees in front of the Grain Bureau Office in Wuxuan, and cut open with a five-inch knife by the local school custodian. The livers and hearts were taken back to the town hall for boiling, and were then shared out.

Individuals made use of the situation. One teacher at Gantang Brigade Elementary School in Menshan heard that eating the heart of a beauty could cure sickness. He duly denounced a lovely young girl of around fourteen. After she had been killed by the mob, he cut out her heart and took it home for dinner. Another individual, the female Vice-Chair of the Wuxuan Revolutionary Committee, was said to have become a culinary connoisseur of male genitals.

> **One of those expelled defended himself with the words: 'Cannibalism? It was the landlord's flesh! The spy's flesh!' He had no regrets whatsoever.**

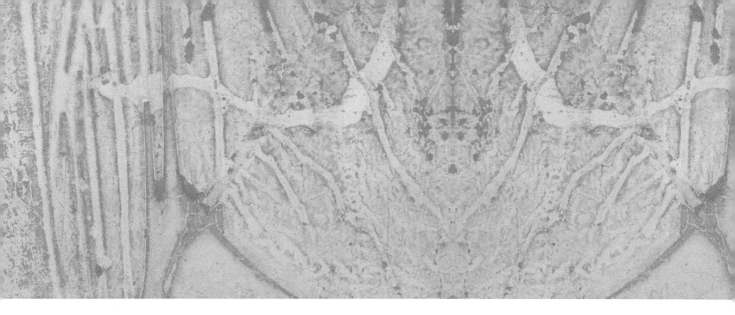

Most of the killings and cannibalism were communal endeavours. In Wuxuan a passer-by from another county was attacked by fifteen locals, killed, cut up and eaten by all of them. When victims were paraded through the town before their executions, women holding empty vegetable baskets lined the street, waiting for their chance to fill them. The *Huangmoo* Food and Supply Store in town was hardly hidden from view, and neither was the eight-foot diameter pot outside, which was used to boil the latest victims of the witch hunt. At least eighty per cent of the locals took part in the feasts. Those who lacked the desire to partake were too afraid to refuse.

A geography teacher in Wuxuan, Wu Shu-fang, was one of those beaten to death for knowing too much. Other teachers were then ordered to drag the body down to the riverbank, and one was forced to cut out the liver, heart and strips of flesh from the thigh. The crowd put these in plastic bags and took them away. Wu Shu-fang was apparently eaten in three places. Seven or eight students consumed some of the flesh in the school kitchen, a casserole was prepared in one of the dormitory rooms, and a third cookery was set up under the roof of an outdoor hallway. A subsequent investigation of this particular incident led to expulsions from the Party but nothing more. One of those expelled defended himself with the words: 'Cannibalism? It was the landlord's flesh! The spy's flesh!' (see Yi, Bibliography). He had no regrets whatsoever.

African civil wars

Africa, of course, had been home to cannibals more recently than most. One famous story concerned Victor Biaka-Bodia, who represented the French colony of Côte d'Ivoire in the French Senate. In 1950, eager to discover what his constituents expected from him, he toured the colony. It turned out they wanted his flesh.

Over the last quarter-century, widespread acts of cannibalism have been reported in several African civil wars. When Liberian President Tolbert was overthrown in 1980, he was disembowelled in his bed but not, apparently, eaten. The man who led the coup, Master-Sergeant Samuel Doe, made lots of promises and failed to keep any of them. He managed to overcome the challenge from Thomas Quiwonkpah – who was eaten – but died under torture in the civil war which began with Charles Taylor's invasion in 1989. The country, meanwhile, had sunk into violent anarchy.

Seven tribal armies, each containing large numbers of frequently drugged child soldiers, ran amok. All the usual restraints of civilization seemed to fall away.

Why this should – in the absence of any serious food shortages – have encouraged cannibalism is an interesting question. The obvious answer is that cannibalism was a far-from-forgotten facet of tribal culture. Repressed in peacetime, it re-emerged phoenix-like from the bloody frenzy of the civil war.

For some, perhaps, it had never gone away. The system of spiritual beliefs known as *poro* has been a mainstay of Liberian culture for centuries. The secrets of the rituals involved are guarded closely, but these rituals certainly involve the use of body parts and probably feature the consumption of human flesh. It seems likely that *poro* includes the usual ideological suspects – transference through consumption and the feeding of gods through sacrifice.

Charles Taylor is reported to have surrounded himself with *poro* witch doctors, drunk the blood of prisoners, and been the leader of a group of cannibals called the 'Top 20'. Taylor denied these allegations, and even sued *The Times* for printing them, but he could not pursue the case for fear of arrest on human rights charges. Whatever the truth of these particular allegations, his country was certainly knee-deep in cannibals during the 1990s. Reporters and refugees witnessed many examples of hearts and

genitals being cut away and eaten, and even the US State Department noted that fighters of all factions 'removed their victims' body parts and ate them in front of civilians' (see Article 2, Bibliography).

Similar stories emerged from the civil war in Sierra Leone, which took off in 1991, and soon descended into the same sort of anarchy. Here, perhaps, the old rituals of the Leopard Societies were given a dust-off and placed at the service of a twentieth-century fight for control of the lucrative industrial diamond trade. One South African mercenary – a less than satisfactory source, perhaps – noted that cannibalism was rife in Sierra Leone. He claimed that prisoners had to be flown to Freetown for interrogation to save them from being eaten, that the tribal warriors used to watch the plane take off and mutter 'there goes dinner' (see Article 1, Bibliography).

The second Congolese civil war, which grew out of the 1994 Rwandan genocide and cost several million lives, also created large areas in which only anarchy and sundry militias ruled. In the early years of the twenty-first century, these seemed to be reliving their ancestral memories, killing and eating their enemies to bolster their own strength. Early in 2003, the UN (United Nations) issued a report condemning these outbreaks of cannibalism. Unfortunately, the Iraq war had just begun and political events soon overtook what attention the report had attracted.

> **Repressed in peacetime, [cannibalism] re-emerged phoenix-like from the bloody frenzy of civil war.**

Aid agencies do vital work in places such as Sierra Leone and Ethiopia. But not all governments will accept outside help

5: Infamous Cannibals Through the Ages

European pioneers

The various civilizations of the ancient world must have had their share of individual cannibals, but their names and particular tastes have been swallowed by the mists of time. The Dark Ages must have boasted a few, if only to live up to their name, and lone cannibals surely stalked the streets of the Crusaders' Jerusalem, the cities of Han Dynasty China, the alleys of medieval London. But no records survive, and their trail of discarded bones has long since disappeared.

The first cannibals

So where do the first cannibal killers make their appearance in the historical record? The almost overly-charismatic figure of Vlad the Impaler seems like a good place to start. Vlad V of Wallachia – to give him his official title – ruled part of what is now Romania in the mid-fifteenth century. He was a cautionary figure to his enemies, and remains one to historians. Wallachia shared a border with Transylvania, the legendary cradle of vampirism, and Bram Stoker supposedly used Vlad as his model for Count Dracula, but there is no actual evidence that Vlad himself was prone to

drinking blood. He certainly liked shedding it, and in some style, nailing turbans to the heads of Turkish envoys who failed to remove them, and despoiling at least one scene of outstanding natural beauty by impaling 20,000 of their countrymen on a vast field of sharpened poles. He is also credited with devising one form of social engineering still popular among sections of the rich – eliminating poverty by killing the poor. But was he a cannibal? No one actually knows.

Gilles Garnier admitted to being a werewolf, which was not so unusual in the sixteenth century as it would be today. Whether he and other self-confessed wolf-men really believed in their power to metamorphose, or had simply been tortured into saying so, remains a moot point. Accusers of werewolfery were like accusers of witchery – both relied on fear and prejudice to offset the lack of any real evidence.

Garnier, though married, was something of a hermit, with a face 'sufficient to repel any one seeking his acquaintance' (see Anon, Bibliography). He certainly seemed to have killed and eaten several children in the Dôle region of central France around 1573, but the evidence produced at his trial was, like his confession, somewhat lacking in credibility. During that summer

Gilles Garnier admitted to being a werewolf, which was not so unusual in the sixteenth century as it would be today.

Lucas Cranach the Elder's compelling 16th-century image of a werewolf reveals the belief in, and the horror attached to, such beings at the time

Good riddance: the grisly end to the Bedburg werewolf, Peter Strubbe, could not have been more fitting

a number of mutilated and half-eaten bodies had turned up, along with sitings of a wolf-like creature who, witnesses claimed, bore a marked resemblance to the hermit. Early in November, some peasants on their way home from work had interrupted an attack on a small girl, and while some claimed the attacker had been wolf-like, others swore it was Garnier.

More ravaged bodies had shown up in the weeks that followed, and eventually Garnier – in wolf-form – was seen and

was in. In 1574 he was successfully burned at the stake, thus refuting later claims that werewolves can only be dispatched by a silver bullet.

...after tying him to a wheel his executioners cut away pieces of flesh with red-hot pincers, broke his bones with clubs and cut off his head and burned the body.

At the time of Garnier's execution a German contemporary named Peter Stubbe was nearing the halfway point of a depressingly prolific career: he terrorized the area of Bedburg for almost a quarter of a century, raping, murdering and eating scores of women and young children. In his torture-assisted confession he claimed to have attacked his victims in the form of a wolf, but to have reverted to human form for the rapes and murders. He admitted pulling unborn babies from their mother's wombs and eating their hearts 'panting hot and raw' (see Martingale, Bibliography). He also consumed his son by his own daughter, allegedly finding the boy's brains 'most savoury and delicious' (see Martingale, Bibliography). Stubbe's

recognized attacking another child. Arrested, he confessed to tearing several children apart with his teeth and wolf's paws, eating parts of the bodies and taking other joints home to his wife. He claimed that the urges to kill and eat human flesh were always with him, whichever mode he

confession might seem a little over-exaggerated, but it ensured him of a commensurate death: after tying him to a wheel his executioners cut away pieces of flesh with red-hot pincers, broke all his bones with clubs, cut off his head and burned the body.

The lesson would have been lost on Countess Elisabeth of Bathory. A distant Hungarian relation of Vlad the Impaler, the Countess was married at fifteen to a castle-owning aristocrat named Count Ferencz Nadasy, and spent most of the succeeding twenty-eight years thinking up new forms of sadistic violence to try on the servants. Her husband and aunt helped provide the inspiration: he with his encyclopaedic knowledge of Turkish torture techniques, she with her penchant for using the flagellation of buxom peasant girls to turn herself on. Armed with a burning torch and her trusty pair of flesh-tearing pincers, the Countess killed and maimed more at less at will. As long as she stuck with peasant girls, the risk was minimal; the state was not there to restrain the aristocracy.

When her husband died in 1604, the Countess began looking for his replacement, but her age and – one would like to think – character made her a less than enviable proposition. How could she make herself more attractive? A servant girl unwittingly supplied the answer, spraying blood on the countess' face when slapped. Washing the blood off, the

Once the victim was dead, the flesh was sometimes fed to local peasants – and future victims

Countess noticed that the area of skin which had received the dousing looked more youthful than the rest. The lesson was clear. She needed blood, and lots of it.

The local peasant girls supplied the necessary. Daily baths in the red elixir required a lot of blood, and the castle servants must have spent most of their lives on wider and wider sweeps of the surrounding countryside. The unfortunate victims were drained, at first by conventional methods, and later with the aid of an iron maiden. This was a box moulded into human shape, its interior lined with sharp spikes. When closed, the spikes pierced the flesh, causing blood to flow from the still-living victim through a hole in the bottom. Once the victim was dead, the flesh was sometimes fed to local peasants – and future victims.

At least, this is how the legend goes. Reay Tannahill points out that a human body only contains a gallon of blood, 'barely enough for a sponge-down' (see Tannahill, Bibliography), and that blood is also highly prone to coagulation. So the Countess would have had severe logistical difficulties in arranging a decent bath.

If true, this was the least of her problems. Much more seriously, the blood was not working – she still looked like a psychopathic old woman. Potential

A myth or a murderess? The countess' civilized exterior belied a thoroughly uncivilized woman – to European eyes, at least

salvation only arrived with a local forest sorceress who pointed out the obvious – she needed noble blood for her noble skin. The Countess duly arranged for twenty-five daughters of the minor nobility to attend her newly-established charm school, and set about draining them. The bodies were tossed over the castle wall for the wolves.

Unfortunately for the Countess, the local peasants found them first. The bodies were reported to the authorities, who realized that a real crime – torturing and killing the nobility – had been committed. The military showed up at the castle, found blood and corpses everywhere, and arrested the indignant Countess. Subsequent investigations revealed that she was responsible for the death of over 600 girls. She was tried and found guilty in 1611, but the worst punishment her fellow aristocrats could bring themselves to inflict was confinement in a single room of her own castle. Her lower-class accomplices were publicly tortured and burned alive.

Scottish cannibals

The Scots are rightly famous as engineers, but deserve more than a mention for their pioneering work as cannibals. When Roman Britain was invaded from the north in AD 367, one of the sundry groups involved was an allegedly cannibalistic tribe from Argyll called the Attacotti. They

Some were hung on hooks for imminent consumption, but Mrs Beane was also a dab hand at pickling parts in brine.

later changed sides, but whether their new Roman overlords encouraged them to eat the imperium's enemies is unknown. Back in Scotland meanwhile, their habits lingered on. The Moss Troopers of the border country were said to be fond of eating the flesh and drinking the blood of their enemies, and to have boiled one noble opponent for soup. One individual, the fearsomely named Christie o'the Cleek, was renowned for his love of human flesh, and the hooked axe or 'cleek' with which he yanked his victims from their ponies. Most famous of all, however, were Sawney Beane and his prodigious brood.

The facts about Sawney Beane are hard to pin down. According to some sources, he was active in the early fifteenth century; according to others, it was as late as the early eighteenth century. The account of those who eventually arrested him – and noticed pistols in his cave – suggests the latter date.

Everyone agrees that this Mr Beane was born near Edinburgh. He married a local girl – 'a woman vicious as himself' (see Marriner, Bibliography) – and earned a paltry living digging ditches and cutting hedges. Work was not really what he had in mind, though. He and his wife wandered south-west, finally settling in a rent-free cave complex on the coast of Galloway. But how to earn a living? Cattle-rustling was one possibility, but most of the cattle belonged to the rich, and they

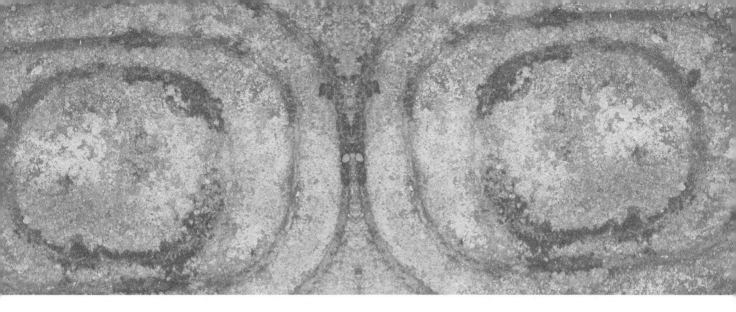

took property rights very seriously. The nearby coast road was not exactly busy, but it did boast enough traffic to support at least one highway brigand. For the next ten years or so Beane and his wife raised a growing family on the proceeds of murder and robbery.

Their reasons for moving into cannibalism are not known. The most likely was the simple attraction of free meat. The bodies were available, and sometimes they must have been hungry. It might even have occurred to them that in eating their victims they were also disposing of the evidence.

Whatever their reasons, the Beanes evolved into a cannibal clan. According to later accounts they sired fourteen children in all, who incestuously sired an improbable thirty-two grandchildren. And they hunted in packs. Small parties and single travellers would find themselves surrounded by Beane males, murdered and taken back to the cave for butchering by Beane females. Some were hung on hooks for imminent consumption, but Mrs Beane was also a dab hand at pickling

Christie o'the Cleek was renowned for his love of human flesh, and the hooked axe...with which he yanked his victims from their ponies.

parts in brine. The victims' cash and possessions were probably used to add some variety to the clan's daily diet. Some bread and vegetables perhaps, or even animal meat.

Hardly surprisingly, the Galloway coast road earned something of a bad reputation, and when a series of amputated limbs washed up on the Galloway coast, the authorities finally took some action. They rounded up the usual suspects – usually the innkeeper who had seen the missing traveller off – and executed them. This reduced the local reputation for hospitality, but did nothing to halt the mysterious disappearances.

The Beanes were eventually interrupted in mid-feast, sucking on the blood of a woman they had just murdered. The fortunate arrival of an armed band drove them off, saving the dead woman's husband from a similar fate. He carried the news to Glasgow, and the Provost – some say the King – organized a manhunt with bloodhounds. The latter led 400 soldiers to the Beanes' cave. It was not a pretty sight. 'They were all so shocked at what they beheld, that they were almost ready to sink into the Earth. Legs, Arms, Thighs, Hands, and Feet of Men, Women and Children were hung up in rows, like Dried Beef. A great many Limbs lay in Pickle, and a great Mass of Money, both Gold and Silver, with Watches, Rings, Swords, Pistols, and a large quantity of Cloaths, both Linnen and Wollen, and an infinite number of other Things, which they had taken from those they had murdered, were thrown together in Heaps, or hung up against the Sides of the Den' (see Johnson, Bibliography).

The Beanes were taken to Leith *en masse*. Their crimes had produced such an outpouring of communal revulsion that a trial was considered unnecessary. The males, their hands and feet cut off, were allowed to bleed to death. The females were forced to watch, and then burned in several large bonfires.

They served to inspire at least one other Scot: Nichol Brown was tried and executed in the mid-eighteenth century for murdering and consuming his wife. At his trial, one witness recounted how Brown had been heard drunkenly outlining his plan to eat the body of a criminal still hanging from a neighbourhood gibbet. Later that evening, he returned with a piece of flesh from the dead man's thigh and cooked it on the pub fire.

Pierce killed Cox with an axe, ate part of him that night, and cut up the greatest part of his flesh in order to take with him.

His companions had the distinct and unwelcome impression that this was not the first time he had tasted human flesh.

Contrasting Frenchmen

Blaize Ferrage Seye was probably a contemporary of Nichol Brown. Born in 1757, he lived his short life in the Cominges region of south-western France, which lies between Toulouse and the Pyrénées. He became a stone mason in his teens, but was soon chased out of his village by a jealous husband. Heading for the hills, he settled, like Sawney Beane before him, in a convenient cave.

Seye seems to have shared Beane's disdain for honest work, preferring to survive on a stolen diet. This only comprized chickens and cattle at first, but Seye soon demonstrated his propensity for extreme violence, abducting, killing and raping – in that order – several young women. When the local farmers made it harder for him to steal animals, he graduated to people, consuming an unknown number of men and women. The authorities found his cave in 1782, and organized a typically brutal execution. The 25-year-old Seye was broken on a wheel, then hung on a gibbet to die of exposure.

His cannibal compatriot Antoine Langulet was a much nicer man. He grew up poor in the Paris of the early nineteenth century, and, according to one rather dubious theory, never got used to a normal diet. He supposedly liked his food rotten, a preference which entailed much hunting through dustbins and the occasional thrill of finding a dead cat. At

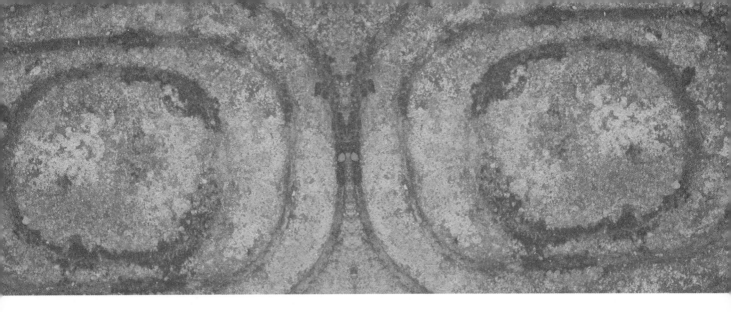

some point in his sad existence, it must have occurred to Langulet that the cemeteries were full of the sort of food he liked, and he embraced the new nocturnal hobby of digging up graves. At first he simply took what he needed – intestines were an unusual favourite, even for a cannibal – and reburied the body for future visits, but soon he was taking the whole lot home. One disinterred young woman required two trips, on the second of which he was challenged by a policeman. In prison, Langulet freely admitted to his activities, and wondered out loud what he had done wrong. He had hungered for the flesh of a young child, he said, but he would never have dreamed of murdering one.

A meal down under

Alexander Pierce, an Irishman from Fermanagh, was sentenced to transportation for stealing a pair of shoes in 1820. He ended up in a harsh convict camp in Tasmania (then called Van Diemen's Land). Several out-of-camp stints as servant to the local dignitaries ended in whippings; an ambitious attempt at forgery proved equally unsuccessful. Pierce was sent back to the camp.

He soon escaped with seven others.

Tasmania was not the easiest of places to traverse on foot, particularly if kangaroo skin jackets were your only source of food. After ten days of mounting hunger, the subject of cannibalism was finally broached, and greeted with a marked lack of enthusiasm. Three men slunk off in the night, leaving the other five to draw lots on who should be consumed. The loser's heart was cut out, fried and eaten. Or this, at least, was what Pierce told the authorities after his recapture. They conceded, somewhat reluctantly, that he might be telling the truth.

He escaped again the following year, this time with a single companion, Thomas Cox. On the second day they reached a wide river. He asked Cox if he could swim, Pierce later told his interrogators. Cox replied that he could not, which did not bode well for their escape plan. This understandably annoyed Pierce, to the point of murder. One thing led to another, and Pierce killed Cox with an axe, ate part of him that night, and cut up the greatest part of his flesh in order to take with him. Recaptured again, Pierce was asked why he had eaten human flesh when he still had supplies of fish and meat. No clear answer was forthcoming, and he was hanged a few days later.

The 19th century

Keeping it in the family

The Pellés – brother Congo and sister Jeanne – lived near the Haitian capital Port au Prince in the mid-nineteenth century. Congo was looking for a career boost that did not involve him in working any harder, and his sister, a voodoo priestess, came up with the obvious solution – a human sacrifice. Their twelve-year-old niece Claircine was chosen for the honour, and duly kidnapped.

A New Year's Eve party was arranged around the sacrifice, complete with would-be consumers and guest priests. One of the latter, a man called Floréal, threw the poor child to the ground and strangled her, then cut off her head with a large knife. The blood was collected in a large earthenware pot, the body flayed and cut up. The skin and entrails were buried in the garden, the rest wrapped up for transport.

The party-goers set off for Floréal's house, holding up the severed head and chanting the appropriate voodoo incantations. Once there, they made preparations for the feast, unaware that their neighbours – curiosity whetted by the aforementioned head and chants – were watching through a chink in the wall. Two courses were prepared – a casserole of flesh and congo beans, a soup of head and yams. The whole party of fourteen partook of the food, then danced and debauched their way into the new year. Come morning, they warmed up the leftovers and had them for breakfast.

The witnesses told their story to the police, who initially had a hard time believing it. Their failure to find Claircine made them less incredulous, and a judicious use of beatings provided the necessary confessions. Of the fourteen arrested, eight were brought to trial. At least one of them, Jeanne Pellé, could not work out what all the fuss was about. 'Why should I be put to death for observing our ancient customs?' (see Marriner, Bibliography) she asked the judge.

All eight were sentenced to death, but executing the voodoo priests and priestesses proved trickier than expected. It took an incompetent firing squad half an hour to finish everyone off, and on the following day three of the graves – those belonging to Jeanne Pellé, Floréal and another voodoo priest – were found to be empty. It is possible that the bodies were carried away for consumption, or that the threesome were never shot in the first place. They might even have staged a voodoo resurrection. One thing was certain: Congo Pellé had no more need to worry about his career.

Vincent Verzeni

If the Pellés seem like an horrific throwback, Vincent Verzeni seems like a ghastly premonition of what was to come. His murderous career took root at the age of twelve, when he discovered that wringing the necks of chickens gave him a sexual buzz. His first human victim was fourteen-year-old Johanna Motta, whom he caught alone in open country. Strangling was no longer enough – 'I took

'Why should I be put to death for observing our ancient customs?'

Voodoo artefacts sum up the cult's less-appealing traits

a great delight in drinking Motta's blood… I took the clothing and intestines, because of the pleasure it gave me to smell and touch them. It never occurred to me to touch or look at the genitals or such things. It satisfied me to seize the women by the neck and suck their blood' (see Krafft-Ebing, Bibliography).

Or so he later claimed. In fact, Motta's genitals had been torn from her body, and there were bite-marks all over her legs where Verzeni had tried to suck blood. A piece of flesh had been cut from a calf for later consumption.

He was not caught, and ten months later he struck again: a married woman this time, again strangled and mutilated. Over the next few years he killed and part-consumed around twenty other women. Verzeni's murderous rampage was only brought to a halt when his cousin Maria successfully fought off his attempt to strangle her.

He was twenty-two at the time. In court he freely admitted his sins, claiming that he was unable to resist the impulse to kill and maim. He begged the judge to remove him from temptation by locking him up for life. The judge was only too pleased to oblige. In later years, Verzeni provided Richard von Krafft-Ebing, the pioneering sexual psychologist, with detailed accounts of his crimes. Strangling, he said, gave him much more sexual pleasure than masturbation. Krafft-Ebing wrote it all down, and decided that drinking blood and eating flesh was just a logical progression from what he called 'lust-murder'. He was the first chronicler of

this particular sickness, and far from the last.

Go West

The nineteenth-century American West seems to have had more than its share of cannibals. There were representatives, moreover, of all the major types.

In April 1838, one group of Pawnees selected a teenage girl for sacrifice. She was paraded through the village, given gifts by each family, and then decorated in garments and feathers of red and black. The girl was then roasted alive on an open fire, while the men pierced her with arrows to draw blood. At the chosen moment, the witch doctor cut out her heart and ate it. The body was then cut up, and the pieces of flesh squeezed dry of blood on the newly planted grain. The flesh that remained was turned into a paste and smeared on the root vegetables. The tribe's future supply of food had been guaranteed.

No one knows how common such cultural-cannibalistic ceremonies were in the nineteenth-century American West, and no one has been that eager to find out. Over recent years most historians and anthropologists have been happy to concentrate on the more eco-positive aspects of Native American culture, and human sacrifice still warrants a bad press.

Many Native Canadian tribal legends featured the werewolf (the *wendigo* in the local parlance). In 1879, a Cree named Katist Chen was either visited by one – the generous explanation – or, as most people thought, he evoked the legend to justify his

A lot of Native American tribes followed similar traditions to those of the Aztecs to ensure a good harvest. Pawnee Indians (woman, right) also practised human sacrifice to please the gods, and the ritual cannibalization of that gift

The pistol believed to have been used by Packer to kill Bell, after Bell killed the other four members in their party and attacked Packer with a hatchet. The painting in the backgound shows Packer defending himself

crimes. These consisted of murdering and eating his mother, wife, brother and six children during a hunting expedition. Chen's claim at his trial that they had all starved to death was dismissed, and he was sentenced to hang. Waiting in prison for his execution, he told a priest that he had killed his family while possessed by a *wendigo*. He claimed only to be confessing at this late date because the *wendigo* had visited him in jail and tortured it out of him.

Just before reaching the Agency they noticed some discarded pieces of what looked like strips of human flesh.

The non-Native Americans had their cannibals too: the Donner party's descent into survival cannibalism and worse has already been recounted. Around the time Katist Chen was killing his family on the other side of the 49th parallel, a trapper named Jeremiah Johnson was bidding for the title as the world's most prolific consumer of human livers. Johnson, who had come out west to get away from civilization, set up house in Montana with an Indian wife and child. When these were

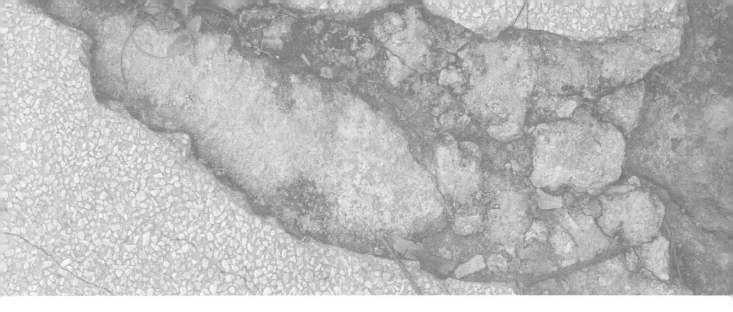

killed by Crow Indians, he waged a one-man war on the tribe, attacking their camps with the sort of monomaniacal zeal that guaranteed eventual immortalization on celluloid. He butchered all the resultant corpses, ate and apparently counted all the livers – 247 of them. His neighbours expressed their disapproval of this retrograde habit by electing him sheriff.

Until Robert Redford played Jeremiah Johnson in the eponymous movie, the most infamous white cannibal of the American West was Alferd[sic] G. Packer. Famous '60s folk-singer Phil Ochs wrote a song about him, and Colorado University students named their dining room in his honour. He was also the recipient of a wonderful comic epitaph: 'There were only seven Democrats in Hinsdale County,' his trial judge told him, 'and you ate five of them, you depraved Republican son of a bitch!' (see Marriner, Bibliography).

In the autumn of 1873, Packer agreed to guide a party of nineteen gold prospectors into the San Juan Mountains of western Colorado. He was in his mid-twenties, already a veteran of the Union Army, and supposedly knew the area inside out. If so, his decision to leave for the high country in autumn seems rather strange.

For several weeks the party headed south-eastwards from their Salt Lake City starting point. They found no gold, but did manage to lose some of their supplies in a botched river-crossing. Winter was fast approaching, and the whole party was close to starvation when they stumbled, by luck, into Chief Ouray's Gunnison Valley camp. The white men feared the worst, but these Indians had obviously forgotten what feeding the Pilgrim Fathers had done for their eastern cousins. They gave Packer and his party all they could spare, and earnestly entreated them to give up their folly while they still could. Ten listened, and headed back to Salt Lake City. The nine who refused to abandon their gold fixation were advised to follow the course of the Gunnison River.

Packer had other ideas. The party's intended destination was near the source of the Rio Grande, and he claimed he knew a short cut across the mountains. Four of his nine followers decided they should stick with Ouray's advice, but five took the fatal decision to follow Packer. They only had two days' worth of food, and a blizzard soon brought them to a hungry halt. For a while they lived on rosebuds and pine gum, which probably taste worse than they sound. Either way, they were not enough to live on.

Of the four who followed Ouray's advice, two died of starvation. The other two reached the Los Pinos Indian Agency in February 1874, more than half-starved but still alive. The Agent Charles Adams supervised their recovery before sending them back down to civilization. Packer showed up a month later, alone. He also pleaded for food, but he did not look that hungry. In fact, he looked almost bloated for someone who said he had spent the winter eating rosebuds and pine gum. When Adams asked him what had happened to his companions, he said they had deserted him. Adams was suspicious, but he had no way of disproving the story. He fed Packer and let him go.

The evidence Adams needed trickled in over the next two months. Packer himself was one witness. He failed to discard guns and knives which were later recognized as belonging to the other members of his group, and he let slip a stream of interesting details while drunk in public. He did not let the whole cat out of the bag, but its ears and tail were certainly showing.

This was enough for Adams to have him arrested, but a second piece of evidence was provided by visiting Indians. Just before reaching the Agency, they noticed some discarded pieces of what looked like strips of human flesh. Adams put two and two together – Packer had dumped his supply before coming in. Adams confronted Packer with the pieces of flesh.

Packer may not have been the brightest person ever, but he had had plenty of time to work out a story. The other five had indeed been killed, he said, but he had

'One day Bell said: "I can stand it no longer!" and he rushed at me like a famished tiger, at the same time attempting to strike me with his gun. I parried the blow and killed him with a hatchet.'

only killed one of them, and that in self defence. The first man, Swan, had been killed while he, Packer, was out gathering wood, and was already being cut up for consumption when he returned. The food had not lasted long, and Packer himself had suggested that another man, the corpulent Miller, should be next. One of the others had split his skull with a hatchet. Two more men had gone the same way, leaving only Packer and a man named Bell. 'One day Bell said: "I can stand it no longer!" and he rushed at me like a famished tiger, at the same time attempting to strike me with his gun. I parried the blow and killed him with a hatchet' (see Marriner, Bibliography).

It seemed like a good story until a painter named Reynolds came across the five bodies during a search for picturesque slices of wilderness. Five of them were lined up in a row, each with the breast gouged out to the ribs. Four of the men had been shot in the back of the head; the fifth, Miller, had had his skull smashed in with a rifle butt. Packer's story had been a tissue of lies.

He escaped before charges could be

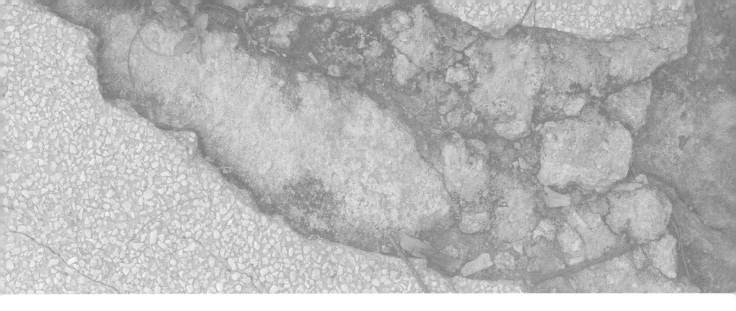

brought, and spent at least some of the next nine years living the outlaw life in Wyoming. He was eventually recognized by another gold prospector, arrested, and brought back to Lake City, Colorado for trial. His story had been rearranged to accommodate the known facts, but he still insisted that he had only killed the one man, and that in self-defence. The jury found him less than credible, and voted for the death penalty, but Packer was not finished yet. An appeal was granted, the execution stayed, a retrial ordered. This time he was sentenced to forty years on five counts of manslaughter, but only served seventeen. He always swore he was innocent, but when forensic scientists re-examined the skeletal remains in 1989, they found that the four men had all been shot with the same gun – Packer's.

Fin du siècle

Jack the Ripper shared Vincent Verzeni's liking for mutilation, but the evidence for his being a cannibal is slight. After the fourth of his five known murders, he sent half of his victim's liver to the chairman of the Whitechapel Vigilance Committee, together with a brief but illuminating note: 'T'other piece I fried and ate it was very

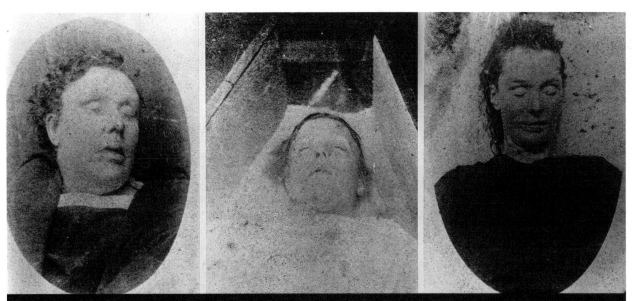

From left to right: Annie Chapman, Mary Ann Nicholls and Elizabeth Stride. Elizabeth Stride was one of two women murdered by the Ripper on the same night

One of many letters written to the police during the 1880s, purporting to be from Jack the Ripper

nise' (see Martingale, Bibliography).

Adolph L. Luetgert was not a cannibal at all, but he was one of cannibalism's great facilitators. He emigrated to the United States from Germany in 1870 at the age of twenty-one, suffused with the desire to become a leading sausage-maker. It did not take him long to live the dream – by 1873 the sausages from his Chicago factory were famous throughout Illinois, particularly among other immigrants of central and east European extraction.

Luetgert lived the good life for the next couple of decades, showering his ample profits on his increasingly ample frame and numerous mistresses. The only cloud was his wife Louisa, who kept telling him that his neglect of the business would drive them into bankruptcy. This led to an increasingly unhappy marriage, and on one occasion he chased her down the street brandishing a revolver.

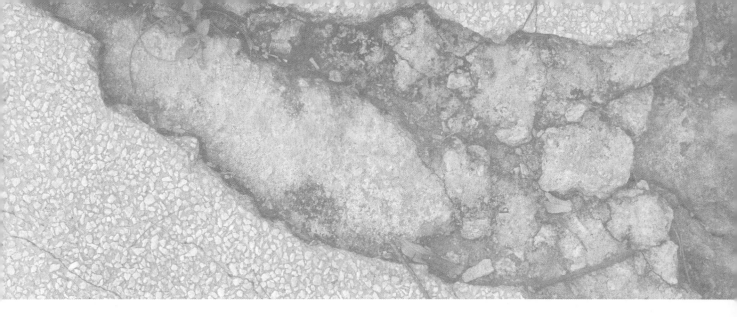

And then, early in May 1897, Louisa disappeared. Luetgert tried and failed to convince his mother-in-law that publicity would damage his standing as a pillar of the community, and an inquiry got underway. Louisa, it turned out, had last been seen alive on 1 May, with her husband, on the street which ran beside his factory. On that very night, the factory nightwatchman remembered the boss sending him out on several unnecessary errands. And, on the following morning, another employee had been offered a job for life when he pointed out that one of the vats contained slivers of bone and a patina of brown slime.

All of which looked extremely suspicious. There was, however, no body and no proof. Luetgert suggested his wife might have gone back to Germany. The police decided to drain the four vats. In the bottom of one they struck pay dirt – a metal corset clip, bone fragments, teeth, and a gold ring engraved with Louisa's initials. Luetgert blustered. The bone fragments and teeth were from pigs, he said. The ring could have belonged to anyone with the same initials. Louisa, he added, could never got hers off her fat fingers.

One by one, his arguments were demolished. Louisa's dentist and mother identified the teeth and ring respectively; a pathologist certified that the bones were human. The ring had come off her fat finger as the flesh dissolved in the boiling sausage meat. There was no body because it had been eaten by Luetgert's customers. He was given a life sentence in Joliet.

Some historians say that the real twentieth century began in 1914. If so, the Hungarian Bela Kiss was the last famous cannibal of the nineteenth. In the two years before the First World War he strangled around twenty women in his village just outside Budapest. He drank their blood in classic Dracula-style, leaving puncture marks on the necks. Each bloodless body was crammed into its own metal drum for pickling in alcohol. He told the local police that his growing drum collection was for stockpiling gasoline in case of war.

This was unfortunate. Kiss was called up in 1914, and the police, on requisitioning his spare gasoline, got a bit of a shock when they unsealed the drums. Hearing of the discovery, Kiss faked his own death by switching identity papers with a dead comrade. Though recognized on several occasions in the ensuing years – once in Hungary and twice in New York City – he somehow managed to evade capture.

The German quartet

There is no doubt that times were hard in Germany after the First World War. By the time hostilities ended, the British blockade had created a serious food shortage, and the imposition of huge financial penalties effectively stymied any German economic recovery. Inflation gathered pace, wiping out middle class savings and scruples. On the streets huge numbers of bitter ex-soldiers fought each other in the name of either communism or the new fascism. German society was splitting asunder, and a plethora of evils came oozing out between the cracks. Hitler and the Nazis were one; Germany's notorious quartet of cannibals were another.

The meat merchant

Georg Karl Grossmann was the first to feel the hand of the law on his shoulder, and probably the first to set up shop. He was born in Neuruppin, a small town some fifty miles north-west of Berlin, in 1863, and seems to have spent a fair portion of his adult life answering police questions about illicit relationships with children and animals. At some point in his life he acquired some skill as a butcher, but whether or not he actually worked as one is open to question. We know that in 1913 he rented a flat near Berlin's Silesian Station, and that he planned to pay his way through begging and selling meat on the street. He only agreed to take the flat when the landlord granted him exclusive use of a kitchen and his own separate entrance.

People said that Grossmann was a burly, surly man, but he could also turn on the charm. Now in his fifties, he rarely lacked for female company. When he turned to killing that company is also unknown – he may have turned to human butchery only towards the end of the war, when animal meat became increasingly hard to get hold of.

His *modus operandi* was simple enough. He would wander down to the Silesian Station to meet the trains from the east. These, particularly after the war, would have their share of young, naive country girls who had come to the city in search of work. Grossman would pick out the plump ones, tip his hat and ask if they needed assistance. He would hint that he needed a housekeeper, and offer them lodgings for a night or two while they got their bearings in the big and frightening metropolis. A couple of days later, he would be pickling joints of their flesh or grinding it into sausages for selling in the local markets. There is no suggestion that Grossmann ate the flesh himself. He turned his customers into unknowing cannibals, and made a

> **A couple of days later, he would be pickling joints of their flesh or grinding it into sausages for selling in the local markets.**

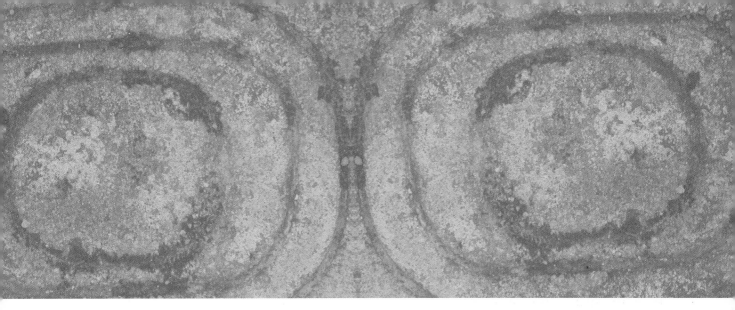

good profit on the deal. Retribution finally came in August 1921. Other tenants in the building heard the sounds of a violent struggle coming from Grossmann's flat and called the police. They arrived to find the trussed-up carcass of one young woman laid out in the kitchen ready for butchering, along with the dismembered remains of three other bodies. The names of many other victims were listed in Grossmann's diary.

He was sentenced to death by the standard German method of that era – beheading with an axe. Perhaps that seemed a little too much like butchery – Grossmann used his braces to hang himself in his cell.

The model citizen

More is known about Karl Denke. He was born in 1870, the second son of a reasonably prosperous farmer in what was then German Silesia. A poor student, he became an apprentice gardener at the age of twelve, and made a living that way until his father died in 1895. He used the resulting inheritance to buy a small farm and garden just outside the small Silesian town of Münsterberg (now the Polish town of Ziebice).

Farming proved beyond him, and he

> ...he may have turned to human butchery only at the end of the war when animal meat became increasingly hard to get hold of.

eventually swapped the farm for a two-storey house in town. He took lodgers and lived off his savings, acquiring a reputation as one of the town's most respectable citizens. Papa Denke, as he was affectionately known, neither drank nor ran after women. His only obvious vice – one that many considered a virtue – was playing the church organ on Sundays.

The First World War and its aftermath proved difficult for Papa Denke. His savings were eaten up by inflation, and his rental income disappeared when he had to sell the house. He stayed on as a tenant of the new owner, however, and persuaded his friends in the local authority to grant him a vending licence. Between 1921 and 1924, he built a flourishing business selling leather goods and 'boneless pork'. He also did his Christian duty, offering hospitality to any young vagrants who passed through the town.

Or so it seemed. On 21 December 1924, one of two things happened. According to one account his upstairs neighbour – a coachman named Gabriel – heard cries for help through the floor. Rushing downstairs, he found a young man with a bleeding head who claimed that Denke had attacked him with an axe. The police were called. Another, more credible account had the young man turning up at the police station and bleeding all over their counter. According to this second account, the police, unable to shake the young man's story, went off, somewhat reluctantly, to collect the town's model citizen. Denke was put in a holding cell while the cops tried to work out what to do with him. They needn't have bothered. At 11.30 that evening their prisoner was found dead in his cell, having hanged himself with a handkerchief.

There was now no need to hurry the investigation, and the police waited until relatives had claimed the body before visiting Denke's apartment. They were stunned by what they found, not to say nauseated. The model citizen had two tubfuls of human flesh pickled in brine, pots of human fat and a boxful of bones ready for grinding. There was a machine for making soap and an entire wall hung with belts, braces and shoelaces made from human skin. The police found twelve ID cards belonging to vagrants, and remains of a further eighteen victims.

There was no need to piece the information together – Denke had done it for them, compiling a detailed ledger in which the name, weight and date of death of each victim had been scrupulously listed. It was perhaps this Teutonic thoroughness which inspired another German, the communist poet and playwright Bertolt Brecht, to satirize Denke's accomplishments thus: 'I contend that the best people of Germany, those who condemned Denke, failed to recognize the qualities of true German genius which the fellow displayed, namely: method, conscientiousness, cold-bloodedness, and the ability to base one's every act on a firm philosophical foundation. They should have made him a Ph.D. with honours' (see Askenasy, Bibliography).

The butcher of Hannover

Fritz Haarmann was born in Hannover on 25 October 1879, the sixth and last child of a railway foreman and his much older wife. Frau Haarmann never really recovered from the birth, and spent most of her remaining twelve years in bed. She did not blame Fritz though, and he was deeply devoted to her. His father, by contrast, was a drunken, womanizing bully who beat both Fritz and his mother – hardly a positive masculine role model. Not altogether surprisingly, Fritz grew up with a liking for dolls and a penchant for dressing in his sisters' clothes.

At the age of sixteen, the young Haarmann was refused a locksmith apprenticeship, and decided instead to enlist in a military training school for NCOs (non-commissioned officers). This went well at first, but a gymnastics accident gave him concussion and

Bones dumped by Haarmann in the River Leine. They, and many others, were found after it was dredged for evidence

triggered a series of epileptic fits. Back in Hannover, he indecently assaulted a number of young children, and was examined at the local asylum. The doctors pronounced him 'feeble-minded' and not really responsible for his actions.

He escaped a few months later and spent several months in Switzerland, honing an ability to live off petty crime. Returning home, he seems to have made one last stab at normal life, courting and marrying a respectable girl named Erna. He could not keep up the pretence, though, soon abandoning his wife and their unborn child for the army. His year or so in the 10th Jaeger Battalion seems to have been

He haunted the main railway station, picking out young male arrivals whom he found sexually attractive, and using his police badge to question them. If it seemed like someone would come looking for a particular boy, Haarmann would let him go.

the happiest of his life, but his superiors eventually came to the same conclusion as the asylum doctor – he was pronounced 'mentally deficient' and discharged. He returned to Hannover and his hated father, who tried to have him committed. The authorities were unconvinced, and Haarmann settled into a life of crime. He would spend almost half of his remaining twenty years in prison, making amends for various acts of robbery, fraud and indecent assault.

He was spared any involvement in the First World War by a five-year sentence for fraud, re-emerging in 1918 to discover a Germany that might have been made for him – anarchic, atomized, desperate. He was soon involved in a meat-smuggling ring, covering his bets by acting as a police informer or *spitzel*. His criminal and police acquaintances tended to think of him as stupid but harmless, and a pleasant enough fellow all-in-all. And what a lot of tips he provided: the cops started calling him Detective Haarmann, and loaned him a badge to use when questioning people on their behalf.

Haarmann's first known victim was Friedel Roth, a seventeen-year-old runaway whom he picked up at Hannover Station. He took the young man back to his rooms on Cellerstrasse, seduced or raped him, killed him by biting through his windpipe, drank his blood and sodomized the corpse. Some of the latter ended up as reasonably priced joints on his market stall, the rest in the watery depths of the River Leine.

Friedel's parents came looking, and

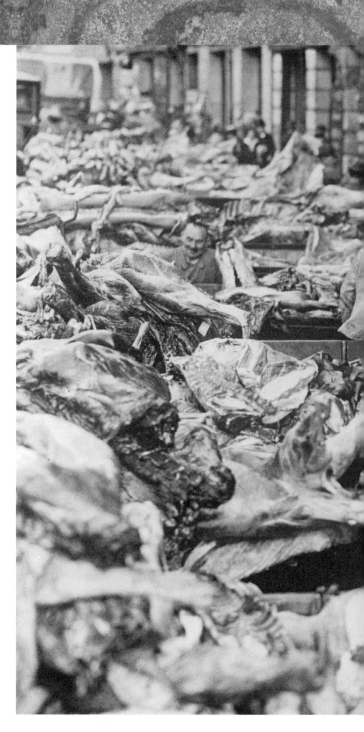

found witnesses who had seen their son with Haarmann. The police reluctantly agreed to question their popular informer, and found him in bed with a young boy. Haarmann was sentenced to nine months, but it could have been much more. According to Haarmann, Friedel's head was sitting behind the oven, wrapped in a newspaper.

A butchers' market in early twentieth-century Hannover. It would have been all too easy to cover the origins of any meat sold

Released in September 1919, Haarmann moved into a new apartment at 8 Neustrasse and took up where he had left off. He haunted the main railway station, picking out young male arrivals whom he found sexually attractive, and using his police badge to question them. If it seemed like someone would come looking for a particular boy, Haarmann would let him go. If not, he took him home and killed him.

Except, that is, for Hans Grans, whom Haarmann took for a partner. Grans was the twenty-year-old son of a librarian, a pimp and petty thief by choice rather than circumstance, and utterly devoid of a conscience. It seems unlikely that he shared in the actual killing, but he played

[Haarmann] denied killing one boy because he was too ugly, and described with some relish how he bit through the throats of others.

a major role in the selection of victims, often picking out particular young men because he liked the look of their clothes.

Grans helped with the dismemberment, with selling the meat and clothes on their market stall, and with dumping the unwanted remains in the River Leine. The neighbours often heard chopping sounds, and occasionally met one of the pair on the stairs with a bucket of blood, but told themselves that the pair were legitimate butchers. One neighbour thought some bones he had been offered were unusually white, but the police were uninterested, and Haarmann made sure thereafter that all the bones went into the river.

This, it turned out, was his major mistake. By early 1924, the number of reported disappearances in Hannover was generating some dark rumours, and when a boy's skull was washed up on the banks of the Leine, some people started putting two and two together. Not the police, of course, who put it all down to public hysteria. A second skull dented their assurance somewhat, and a whole sackful of human remains drove a horse and cart straight through it. The river was dredged, yielding more than five hundred human bones from twenty-seven separate bodies.

Since Haarmann was on first name terms with most of the Hannover police department, detectives were brought in from Berlin to keep an eye on him. They did not have long to wait – a row at the station ended with a young man accusing Haarmann of indecent assault. He and Grans were arrested, their flat searched. There was blood everywhere of course, but that could be put down to their trade. The identified clothes of missing boys were harder to explain, and Haarmann was steered towards a confession by the usual mixture of logic and physical persuasion.

The two men were charged with twenty-seven murders. Haarmann, when pressed, said he could not remember whether it had been thirty or forty. Others put their estimate much higher, closer to 200.

The trial was notable for Haarmann's cruel disregard of the relatives' feelings. He denied killing one boy because he was too ugly, and described with some relish how he bit through the throats of others. Grans, meanwhile, maintained an almost total silence, and was rewarded with a life sentence (later reduced to twelve years). Haarmann demanded execution in the market place where he had sold his meat, but was beheaded behind close doors.

The Düsseldorf vampire

Peter Kurten had the sort of childhood from which few escape unscathed. Kurten Sr had a habit of raping both wife and daughter, and Peter's older brothers spent much of their time in jail. As a nine-year-old he was befriended by the municipal

Once in custody, Kurten was a helpful witness to his own crimes, providing maps to where he had left bodies of his victims

rat-catcher, who enjoyed torturing and sexually abusing animals in front of him. The young Kurten found these experiences stimulating in ways which he could not begin to express or understand. As he got older, he came up with his own twists, stabbing sheep and tearing the heads off swans to drink their blood. It was a taste he would never lose.

In his late teens he attacked two girls, nearly killing one of them, but only received a four-year prison sentence. In later years, he would remember the days spent fantasizing in his cell about all the crimes he would one day commit. Arson came high on the list, because it was so sexually satisfying. Poisoning children with arsenic was another appealing idea. Kurten got intense enjoyment out of inflicting pain.

It seems unlikely that he reached the age of thirty without killing anyone, but his first known murder was committed in 1913. He described his rape and killing of a ten-year-old innkeeper's daughter with detailed relish at his trial seventeen years later, noting that the public horror and indignation 'did me good' (see Askenasy, Bibliography). When war broke out the following year, he was called up, but allegedly deserted on his first day of service. If so, one wonders how he avoided being shot when arrested for yet another arson offence. Instead, he spent a few more years in jail. He was a well-behaved prisoner; however, when he volunteered to help with the laying out of dead prisoners his offer was, unfortunately, accepted.

Kurten did not look like a sadistic vampire. He was fastidious about his appearance, had perfect manners and an easy way with children. Around 1921 it seems he almost lost himself inside this mask. He married, and treated his wife with great gentleness. He got and kept a job. It was only his half-strangled

> **As he got older, he came up with his own twists, stabbing sheep and tearing the heads off swans to drink their blood.**

mistresses who saw the violence still simmering within.

In 1925 his job sent him back to Dusseldorf, to where his troubles had all begun. 'The sunset was blood-red on my return,' he said later. 'I considered this to be an omen symbolic of my destiny' (see Martingale, Bibliography).

He started killing with what seemed an ever-increasing ferocity – animals, children, women and men. He clubbed them, stabbed them, strangled them with his bare hands. The police, following this trail of carnage, could see only one connecting link – the frenzied consumption of blood. The papers called the killer the 'Düsseldorf Vampire', and Kurten's wife was so frightened of becoming a victim of 'the Vampire' that she asked her husband to escort her home from work each night.

Early in 1930 he slashed a five-year-old girl to death, yet a few weeks later he let his last potential victim go, after checking that she did not remember his address. But the girl had tricked him, and Kurten soon realized as much. He confessed to his wife, and persuaded her to give him up for the reward. At his trial he pleaded guilty to nine charges of murder and a host of other crimes. Before his execution, he told his psychiatrist that he hoped to hear, for just a second or two, the sound of blood gushing from his own neck. 'That,' he said, 'would be the pleasure to end all pleasures' (*see* Martingale, Bibliography).

American gothic

Albert Fish

In May 1928 eighteen-year-old Edward Budd advertised for a summer vacation job in the New York *World Telegram*. That same day an elderly man with wispy grey hair knocked on the door of the Budds' apartment at 406 West 15th Street. With his brightly polished shoes, wing-tipped-shirt and silk-lined hat he looked the picture of respectability. He introduced himself as Frank Howard, and claimed that he had a farm on Long Island. If Edward was interested, he would pay him $15 a week.

It was agreed that the family would think it over, and that Frank Howard would

When Grace Budd had sat on his lap, he now informed the girl's parents, 'I made up my mind to eat her.'

return on the following Saturday for their answer. In the event, he sent a telegram saying he could not make it that day, and would come over on the Sunday morning. He arrived with a pail of pot cheese for Mrs Budd, and was invited to have lunch with the family. The Budds' ten-year-old daughter Grace took an instant liking to the old man, and sat in his lap. After giving the older children enough money to visit the cinema, he suggested that Grace accompany him to a birthday party his married sister was hosting that afternoon.

She put on her white communion dress and left hand-in-hand with her new friend.

The family expected her home that evening, and by the following morning were worried enough to call the police. The married sister's address and farm on Long Island both proved fictional. The telegram and pot cheese were traced, but offered no further clues. Over the next few months, the best efforts of police and media failed to find any trace of either Grace Budd or Frank Howard.

Six-and-a-half years later, on 11 November 1934, the Budds received an unsigned letter. The author opened with the story of a 'friend' marooned in China during the famine of 1894: 'So great was the suffering among the very poor that all children under the age of twelve were sold for food in order to keep others from starving…You could go in any shop and ask for steak…Part of the naked body of a boy or girl would be brought out and just what you wanted cut from it.' The 'friend' had returned to the US with a taste for human flesh, which he satisfied by killing and eating two small boys. All of which had inspired the letter's author to emulate him. When Grace Budd sat on his lap, he now informed the girl's parents, 'I made up my mind to eat her' (see Martingale, Bibliography).

He went into details. Some days before taking the girl away, he had purchased a cleaver, saw and butcher's knife from a Manhattan pawnshop, and deposited them with a news vendor for safe keeping. He had picked up the parcel on his way to the subway with Grace, but then almost left it

Grace Budd's confidence and pretty looks probably sealed her fate in Albert Fish's hands on the New York Central train which took them out to semi-rural Westchester. Grace had ducked back onto the train to retrieve it for him.

On reaching the old abandoned family cottage, he had told the girl to pick some flowers while he looked for his (imaginary) sister. Grace had come in to find him naked, had dropped her posy of flowers and screamed out that she would tell her mother. He had grabbed and strangled her, then gone to work with his new tools. He had taken off the head with the cleaver, and carefully drained as much of the girl's blood as he could into an empty paint drum. He had then sawed the body in half and used the butcher's knife to cut up the pieces, some of which he took home wrapped in a cloth. He had cooked them in a stew with carrots and onions, and found them 'sweet and tender'. So tasty in fact that he had made several trips back to fetch more. It had taken him nine days, he wrote, to eat the entire body.

The effect on the Budds can only be imagined. Their only consolation – and a slim one it must have been – was that their daughter's killer had opened himself up to capture. After checking that the handwriting in the letter matched that in the original telegram, the police used a spectroscope to identify a blacked-out logo on the envelope. This led them, by a roundabout route, to a rooming house in West 52nd Street. The landlady linked the Budds' description of Frank Howard to a former tenant named Albert Fish. His signature in the hotel register matched that of the letter-writer. She had no forwarding address for him, but he returned every few weeks to pick up the money which one of his sons sent him on a regular basis. The police watched and waited, and three weeks later a harmless-looking old man turned up. When arrested, he lunged at the detective with a straight razor, and, once handcuffed, was found to have several knives and razors secreted among his clothes.

Once Edward Budd had formally identified him, Albert Fish freely confessed to Grace's murder and consumption. Her bones were found at the cottage in Westchester, a scrapbook of articles about Fritz Haarmann in the rooming house. And that was far from the end of it. Fish confessed to a slew of other crimes, first to the police and then to the psychiatrists who were queuing up for a shot at him. The newspapers joined the enquiry, digging up all they could about his past and speculating at length about his motives.

> **He had cooked them in a stew with carrots and onions, and found them 'sweet and tender'. So tasty in fact that he made several trips back to fetch more. It had taken him nine days, he wrote, to eat the entire body.**

In custody at last: Fish is led into court by detective William King, who captured Fish after a six-year search

Albert Fish, it turned out, had been born and christened Hamilton Fish in 1870. His father, a steamship captain on the Potomac, had died when the boy was only five, and his mother had placed him in a Washington, DC, orphanage while she established herself in work. The family already had more than its share of dysfunction – two close blood relatives died in mental homes, one was an

with anything too serious. In 1898 he married a woman nine years younger than himself, and over the next twenty years the couple had six children. It was not the most normal of marriages, however. After Fish was arrested his ex-wife called him an 'old skunk' and said she had always known 'something like this' would happen (see Martingale, Bibliography).

She left him and the children in 1917,

The police found he had permanently inserted twenty-nine needles into the lower part of his body, some of which were several inches long.

alcoholic, and four more were considered merely crazy – so young Hamilton may well have been cursed with decidedly unfortunate genes. If so, the orphanage gave them free rein. The boy was probably abused; he certainly endured and witnessed a lot of whippings. Unlike most of the boys, he grew to enjoy them. When, at the age of nine, he was finally taken back home, the damage was already done. Nature and nurture had combined to create a monster.

Fish left home at fifteen, and was soon earning a reasonable living as a house painter and decorator. He claimed he was always naked underneath his overalls, and that he got his early kicks from exposing himself to children. Sometimes he paid for sex with children, at others he forced himself on them. There was always an element of sadism involved, but he was careful enough to avoid being charged

running off with a lodger. Fish claimed that he had first killed in 1910, but his children were convinced that her desertion was what had finally sent him off the rails. He never laid a hand on them – on the contrary, he insisted that they lay a hand on him, and beat him with a paddle studded with half-inch nails. They remembered him climbing the hill behind the Westchester cottage and screaming 'I am Christ!' at the full moon.

Fish confessed to many crimes, often in excruciating detail. The police did not believe his claim to have killed around 400 children, and it does seem likely that he exaggerated the number. There seems little doubt, though, that his victims ran into triple figures. Many were black, for the simple reason that a black child's disappearance was less likely to engage the police. Many were tortured before death and part-eaten afterwards. Fish got intense

sexual pleasure from each part of the process, and greatly enjoyed recounting each grisly episode to the police and psychiatrists. He told them he rarely gagged his victims because he liked to hear them scream. He also tried to wrap his crimes in religion. He was following God's orders, castrating boys in a symbolic repeat of Abraham's offering of Joseph. He even claimed to be saving children from the horrors of life.

The psychiatrists could hardly believe what they were hearing. One, a Doctor Wertham, decided that there was 'no known perversion that [Fish] did not practise and practise frequently' (see Martingale, Bibliography). Wertham listed eighteen sexual perversions which Fish had admitted to, including coprophagy (eating faeces), exhibitionism, fetishism of various kinds, sado-masochism, undinism (sex involving urination) and cannibalism. Not all of Fish's habits involved others. The police found he had inserted twenty-nine needles permanently into the lower part of his body, some of which were several inches long. He also expressed a liking for inserting roses into his penis and then eating them, whilst his children remembered his habit of stuffing rags up his anus and setting fire to them.

At his trial, the defence and their psychiatrists argued the obvious, that any man with Fish's proven record of crimes had to be mad. The prosecution brought in psychiatrists of their own. They claimed that Fish knew right from wrong, which made him legally sane. They also claimed, somewhat obscurely, that many prominent people ate faeces. Judge, jury and public were only too pleased to agree with the first supposition, and even Fish joined the baying chorus. He was not insane, he said, just 'queer'. As if to demonstrate this grasp of reality, he told everyone how much he was looking forward to the electric chair – 'the supreme thrill, the only one I have not tried' (see Martingale, Bibliography). As it happened, he was able to enjoy it twice. The first time they pulled the switch on the laughing Fish, the chair was short-circuited by all the needles in his body.

Ed Gein

Inadequate parents loom rather large among twentieth-century cannibals, and few loom larger than Augusta Gein, Ed's mother. Why she married George Gein only she could say, but she certainly seems to have regretted it. Such was the couple's relationship, that their sons Ed and Henry were frequently treated to the sight of their mother sinking to her knees and praying for their father's death.

The family lived on an isolated 270-acre farm some way from Plainfield, Wisconsin. They do not seem to have done much farming though. George drank and did occasional work as a tanner and carpenter; Augusta worked in a grocery store for a while, but then seems to have concentrated on educating her sons in the heartlessness of other women and the bottomless evil of men. For entertainment they were given the Bible. It seemed more reliable than friends.

Nothing much changed until papa died in 1940. By this time Ed was thirty-four, his brother slightly older, and both had long since outgrown mere dysfunctionality. Henry was the next to go, killed by a forest fire in 1944. His death was presumed accidental at the time, but the circumstances – the body was found some distance from the fire with a bruised head – appeared even more suspicious in the

Ed Gein wanted to be a woman and eagerly devoured news of the first sex-change operation. He wanted to cut off his penis but decided dressing up as a woman would be less painful.

light of later events. Ed, many came to believe, had killed his brother to gain sole possession of their mother. If he did, he had little more than a year to enjoy the monopoly of her 'affections' and, when she died in December 1945, something inside

him apparently gave way.

Reports say that he started acting oddly, though how anyone could tell remains a mystery. He sold off a third of the farm acreage, which allowed him to subsist on occasional jobs as a handyman, and sealed off most of the rooms in the rambling farmhouse. He drank a lot of beer, put away the Bible, and started reading books about human anatomy and Nazi medical experiments – a recognizably disturbing

combination. And, having somehow enlisted the help of a feeble-minded local named Gus, he took to robbing the graves of Wisconsin for bodies and body parts. He stored the bodies in a shed behind the farmhouse and ate many of the body parts. Others he used to make clothing, furniture and ornaments. A belt sewn out of nipples and an armchair upholstered with skin and adorned with real arms were only two of his creations. Compared to them, his trophy heads and soup bowl skulls seemed almost conventional.

Sex – and his mother – were at the heart of the matter. Ed Gein wanted to be a woman, and eagerly devoured news of the first sex-change operation. He considered cutting off his own penis, but decided that dressing up as a woman would be less painful. Unlike most men so inclined, Ed Gein was not thinking of clothes. When he dressed up as a woman, he dressed in a female skin, carefully removed from one of his stolen corpses. He even cut off female genitals, stuffing them in knickers which he then put on. So attired, he would either gaze at himself in the mirror or go outside

and leap around in the moonlight.

This went on for several years, until Gus grew even more feeble-minded, and was placed in an old people's home. Deprived of his sidekick, Gein decided that robbing graves was too much like hard work. Either that, or something inside hungered for a change of gear. Whatever the reason, he moved up from the dead to the living. One snowy night in 1954, he waited outside Mary Hogan's bar until all her customers had gone home, and then walked in, put a gun to her head and shot her dead. The police found a pool of blood and not much else. Gein meanwhile was busy on his lonely farm, butchering the body and pondering what he would do with the bits.

Mary Hogan may not have been the first person he killed. Two young girls had gone missing in the area in 1947 and 1953; two men had never come back from a hunting trip in 1952. Parts from around fifteen bodies were subsequently found at the farm, but most of these probably came from graves. If he handled other killings as

> **Ed and Henry were frequently treated to the sight of their mother sinking to her knees and praying for their father's death.**

Ed Gein: The cold face of the murderer and part-consumer of up to eleven people

ineptly as he did his second known murder, then Ed Gein would probably have been caught several years earlier.

He found Bernice Wordern alone in the family hardware store and shot her with a rifle from the sale rack. He then locked up the shop and took her body home in his truck, leaving a half-written receipt for the antifreeze he had purchased on the counter. When her son returned that evening, he found a pool of blood and the sales receipt, proof that Gein had been the only customer that day. While some cops headed for the farmhouse, others picked up Gein, who had come back into town on an errand and been invited to dinner by acquaintances. 'Somebody framed me,' was his somewhat inadequate answer when asked to account for his movements. 'For what?' he was asked. 'About Mrs Worden,' he replied (see Martingale, Bibliography).

By this time the other cops had reached the farmhouse, and most were wishing they had not. Bernice Worden's body was hanging from the kitchen rafters, minus head, genitalia and organs. Her head was later found with hooks attached, ready for hanging. Her heart was in the frying pan.

The stunned cops called in the forensic team. None of them could believe their

Bernice Worden's body was hanging from the kitchen rafters, minus head, genitalia and organs. Her head was later found with hooks attached, ready for hanging.

eyes. Four noses in a cup, two lips on a string, a row of sawn-off women's heads with traces of lipstick. Some lampshades made from human skin – and all in God-fearing Wisconsin.

Gein confessed to the two murders, and thought that there might have been others – his memory was hazy. He happily admitted to the grave robberies, described his dream of becoming a woman, and the ways he had tried to make it come true. He showed no remorse, and little more in the way of understanding. He thought a memory of his mother slitting open a pig and ripping out its entrails was important, but was not sure why. Diagnosed as a schizophrenic, he was committed to a mental institution until such time as he regained his sanity. He was not expected to and never did. Ed Gein died in July 1984, his body taken back to be buried next to his mother.

The modern vampire

'The Acid Bath Murderer'

John George Haigh was born in Yorkshire, England in 1909. His parents, like so many others in this book, were zealous Christians – in their case, Plymouth Brethren. Young John played the organ, sang in the Wakefield Cathedral choir, and received constant instruction in the perils of sin.

The adult Haigh was a chancer, glib and plausible but with less intelligence than the impression he gave. He was a successful advertising copywriter, but preferred the risk of embezzlement to building a career. He worked hard at teaching himself the techniques of fraud and forgery, but not hard enough to avoid

> **He offered McSwann the use of his basement workshop as a bolt-hole, and welcomed him with a head-crushing blow from an iron bar...he then sank his teeth into McSwann's neck and drank his blood.**

several short prison sentences. His cellmates remembered him fantasizing about perfect crimes, and dissolving a dead mouse in an acid bath.

After emerging from prison in 1944, Haigh put his theories to the test. An old acquaintance named Donald McSwann was trying to stay one step ahead of the authorities, who wanted him for their war with Germany. Haigh had once worked in McSwann's amusement arcade, and seems to have seen his chance. He offered McSwann the use of his basement workshop as a bolt-hole, and welcomed him with a head-crushing blow from an iron bar. According to Haigh's later testimony, he then sank his teeth into McSwann's neck and drank his blood. He had already prepared a barrel of acid for dissolving the body, and the resulting sludge was tipped into the sewers below.

Haigh assumed control and effective ownership of the amusement arcade. When McSwann's parents tried to make contact with Donald, Haigh told them their son had gone into hiding in Scotland. He reinforced this claim by taking almost weekly trips north of the border, and posting them forged letters. This presumably grew tiresome, and Haigh must have decided that murder was more simple. He invited the McSwanns to his own house, where he murdered, dissolved and sluiced them out. A few evenings' work forging documents brought him control of the entire family estate, which included five houses and a substantial amount of cash.

This lasted Haigh about three years. During that time he acquired the use of another workshop, this one attached to industrial premises near Crawley in Sussex. In 1947 he invited a young married couple – Archie and Rosalie Henderson – to take a look at it. They disappeared into a new, larger acid bath.

Gift of the gab: a consummate conman, Haigh enjoys a joke with his warder as he enters court on the first day of his trial for murder

Haigh then told Rosalie's brother that the couple had gone to South Africa owing him money, and produced more forged documents to prove it.

His last victim was Olive Durand-Deacon, a 69 year-old widow who lived in Haigh's apartment block, and who made the mistake of telling him she had money to invest. Others were aware of the connection between them, however, and when she disappeared the police dug up Haigh's less-than-satisfactory prison record. A dry-cleaning receipt for Mrs Durand-Deacon's Persian lamb coat was found on the Crawley workshop floor, and a witness in nearby Horsham recognized Haigh as the man who had sold her jewellery. A dredging of the acid bath turned up traces of human bones and Mrs Durand-Deacon's dentures.

Haigh confessed to the murder, and then told the startled police that he had killed the old woman for her blood. While they were still assimilating this information, he calmly added that he had killed eight other people for the same reason, the five mentioned above and three strangers whose names he did not know. He claimed he had been fond of sucking his own blood since childhood, and that a recurring dream had haunted his adulthood: as he walked through a forest of giant crucifixes, they turned into trees, dripping blood. One of the trees turned into a man with a bowl, who would collect the blood and almost offer it to Haigh, before suddenly turning away. It was only when he killed, Haigh said, that the dream allowed him to sup from the bowl.

There is no evidence that Haigh ever drank the blood of his victims, and no intimation of the sexual dysfunctions which usually accompany such blood obsessions. It is quite possible that he invented his vampirism to support an insanity plea. If so, it did not work. He was hanged in August 1949.

The 'Dracula' killer

There is, unfortunately, no shortage of evidence that Richard Trenton Chase drank the blood of his victims. He had been obsessed with the stuff since childhood, and had spent several spells in Sacramento's psychiatric institutions as a result.

Chase started with birds and moved on up through the pecking order, blending the entrails of rabbits, cats and dogs, even slaughtering a cow in a field. The psychiatrists who examined him seem to

He shot her three times, dragged her lifeless body to the bedroom and cut it open. He drank her blood from an empty yoghurt pot and collected more in another container, leaving red rings on the carpet. Only four days later he went further, killing two adults, a six-year-old boy and a 22-month-old baby.

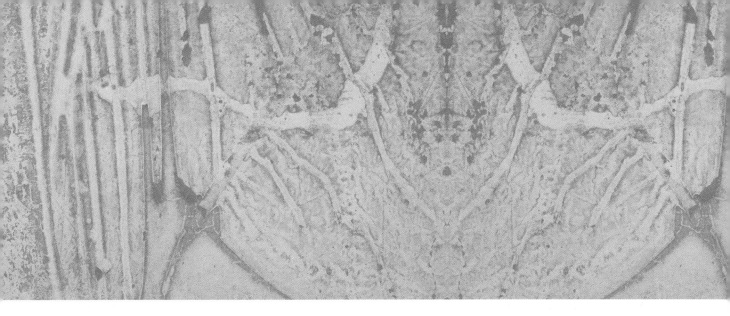

have agreed that something was seriously amiss, but had no apparent compunction about sending him back into the community with instructions to self-medicate. He went home to his hobbies: watching medical dramas on TV and trawling anatomy books for tips on blood collection. Chase was increasingly convinced that he needed transfusions of blood to remain healthy, and by the time he reached his mid-twenties he had taken hypochondria to a whole new level – on one occasion he told hospital doctors that his stomach had turned itself the wrong way round, and that his pulmonary artery had been stolen. The psychiatrist who examined him diagnosed paranoid schizophrenia, but no attempt was made to institutionalize him.

On 27 December 1978, Chase started practising with the .22 handgun he had bought as part of his American birthright. One of his neighbours actually felt a bullet pass through her hair as he tried a pot-shot one day. Two days later, a 51 year-old engineer named Ambrose Griffin was less lucky – he was shot dead between car and house with the groceries he had just brought home. Police were mystified by the apparent randomness of the attack.

They got more evidence than they bargained for a month later. On 23 January Teresa Wallin, a 22 year-old mother-to-be, was carrying garbage to her front door when Chase walked in. He shot her three times, dragged her lifeless body to the bedroom and cut it open. He drank her blood from an empty yoghurt pot and collected more in another container, leaving red rings on the carpet. Only four days later he went further, killing two adults, a six-year-old boy and a 22 month-old baby in another suburban house. All were shot dead before Chase set to work with his knife, draining the blood from the woman's abdominal cavity and cutting open the baby's skull.

Luckily for the other citizens of Sacramento, an old school acquaintance recognized Chase's face on a 'wanted' poster and gave his name to the police. Arrested, he refused to confess to any murders, claiming that the blood strewn around his house was all from animals. He was more honest with his cellmate, who was disgusted enough to pass on the confession. Despite his psychiatric history, the 28-year-old Chase was considered sane enough for trial and execution. He committed suicide in San Quentin Prison, overdosing on a carefully accumulated stash of anti-depressants.

Sons of America

The Co-ed Killer

Ed Kemper's story is utterly horrific, but it sometimes sounds almost too pat, as if the man himself is nothing more than a walking collection of Freudian clichés. His background, his methods and his rituals, his choice of final victim – they seem almost predetermined in their jigsaw neatness. Strange then, that the psychiatrists who examined him and the police who befriended him were the last to recognize the picture.

Edmund Emil Kemper III was born in Burbank, California in December 1948. His parents divorced when he was seven, leaving Ed and his two sisters to live with their mother in Helena, Montana. He was already displaying disturbing behaviour; he hacked the limbs off a sister's doll, and was soon verbalising his inner linkage of sex and death. When his sister asked him why he did not kiss a teacher he had a crush on, Ed replied that if he did, he would have had to have killed her.

He was already huge for his age, and was beginning to scare his sisters, so his mother banished him to a basement cellar that could only be accessed through a trapdoor in the kitchen floor. Not surprisingly, life in his own family prison turned him weirder still. He took his rage out on the family cat, burying it alive. He then dug up the corpse, cut off its head, stuck it on a stick, and took it to his bedroom.

He was entering adolescence now, and his mother decided that she could not cope with him any longer. She sent him to his father, who did not want him either. Between them, they decided that his paternal grandparents might work some sort of miracle. They had a 17-acre farm up in the mountains, and were not the sort of people to take any nonsense. Ed managed almost a year with them, before shooting his grandmother dead in a fit of pique. Two more bullets and a frenzied stabbing later, he sat down to wait for his grandfather. He shot the old man, he said later, to spare him the sight of his wife's body. He then phoned his mother, who advised him to ring the police. He was fourteen years old.

He spent the next five years in a mental hospital. The psychiatrists decided he was paranoid and psychotic, and specifically warned that he should never be released into the custody of his mother. His IQ was found to be well above average, and he proved a model inmate, ever-helpful and always interested. In 1969 his parole board decided he was cured, and sent him back to his mother, who was now living in Santa Cruz, California.

He tried to join the city police, but was rejected on account of his height – Kemper was now six

> **When his sister asked him why he did not kiss a teacher he had a crush on, Ed replied that if he did, he would have had to have killed her.**

'Big Eddie': his appetite to kill was as large as he was

feet nine inches tall, and weighed well over 200 pounds. He hung out with them instead, frequenting the local cops' favourite bar and acquiring the affectionate nickname 'Big Eddie'.

He knew what he wanted to do, and eventually did it. Santa Cruz was a college town, and many of the students hitch-hiked their way around the area. Kemper spent a few weeks offering lifts and practising his charm before picking up his first victims, eighteen-year-old Anita Luchese and Mary Ann Pesce, on 7 May 1972. Their murder, dismemberment and ritualized consumption kept him satisfied for several months, and it was not until September that he struck again, killing a fifteen-year-old Korean-American dance student named Aiko Koo. Eighteen year-old Cindy Schall followed in January, Rosalind Thorpe and Alice Lui (twenty-three and twenty-one respectively) a month later. There seemed nothing to stop him. Kemper's police buddies kept him fully apprised of how the investigation was going – which was not well. The 'Co-Ed Killer' was leaving no clues.

His *modus operandi* hardly varied: Kemper stabbed and strangled his

He tried to put the offending organ down the waste disposal unit, but the machine spat it back out.

District Attourney Peter Chang (right) checks the paperwork on the case that would find Kemper guilty of six murders

victims, prolonging their agony for as long as he could to maximize his own sexual enjoyment. He took the bodies back to his apartment, where he stripped them, posed them in the bath and took polaroid pictures of them. He then dismembered them, starting with the head because he enjoyed necrophiliac sex with the headless corpses. He wrapped the heads in cellophane and kept them as trophies, disposing of the hands and feet, and cutting up the trunk for food. He devised a whole series of recipes, but taste was not the issue. Eating with the polaroids laid out beside his plate was guaranteed to give him intense sexual pleasure. Cannibalizing his victims was Kemper's way of prolonging the intense arousal which had accompanied their murders.

Kemper was a very cool customer – when he attended a hearing on his own sanity at the local court, Aiko Koo's head was in the trunk of his car. The court, almost needless to say, was pleased with his progress. And Kemper was careful – he aborted one killing when he noticed his intended victim's friend noting down his car registration number in the rear-view mirror. He knew his last crime would identify him, but went ahead with it anyway. Perhaps he realized that the other killings were just rehearsals for the real

thing; perhaps he just could not wait any longer.

On 21 April 1973 he walked into his mother's bedroom and beat her sleeping head in with a hammer. He then cut off her head and tore out her larynx. 'This seemed appropriate,' he said. 'As much as she had bitched and screamed and yelled at me over the years.' He tried to put the offending organ through the waste disposal unit, but the machine spat it back out. 'Even when she was dead she was still bitching at me,' Kemper said later. 'I could not get her to shut up' (see Martingale, Bibliography). He propped her head on a hatbox and used it as a dartboard, then had sex with the headless body. Nothing worked. He dumped the body in a cupboard and went out in a rage.

He went back to his mother's apartment and phoned one of her friends, inviting her round for dinner. When she arrived he

death penalty at the time, and was unable to even half oblige him, so Kemper remains alive to this day. In one interview given from prison, he posed himself the question: 'What do you think when you see a pretty girl walk down the street?' His answer was: 'One side of me says I'd like to talk to her, date her. The other half of me says "I wonder how her head would look on a stick"' (see Greig, Bibliography).

House of horrors
Gary Heidnik was two when his quarrelsome, alcoholic parents split up.

> **Bingo and loan sharking paid [his] salary, and the congregation fulfilled his sexual needs, often *en masse*. He used some of the money to play the stock exchange...by 1977 he had accumulated over $35,000.**

went through the familiar ritual, strangling her, beheading her, having sex with the corpse. After sleeping in his mother's bed, he left a note for the cops and headed out east in his victim's car. He was only going through the motions, and was thoroughly annoyed by the lack of headlines which accompanied his flight. In the end he had to phone the police and give himself up. Even then it took three calls to persuade them.

When asked what the appropriate punishment would be for his crimes, Kemper replied, 'Death by torture' (see Greig, Bibliography). California had no

His mother took custody of him and his new-born brother Terry, but soon found she could not cope and handed them back to their father. He was clearly salt of the earth – when Gary persistently wet his bed his father beat him and hung the sheets out of the window to show the neighbours. A fall from a tree gave the boy a slightly misshapen head, earning him the nickname 'football head', and generally added to his misery.

Like Ed Kemper, whose story offers so many points of comparison, Gary Heidnik was a clever boy who never found a way of putting his intelligence to positive use. He

Heidnik was executed by lethal injection in July 1999

did well at his military academy, and joined the regular army at the age of eighteen, in 1961. Despite devoting rather too much energy to loan sharking, he actually seemed to be making a career of the military, until a random neurological test earned him an immediate discharge. The 'schizoid personality disorder' diagnosis earned him a disability pension for life, but seems to have taken away his main reason for living.

Heidnik settled in Philadelphia and drifted from job to job. He qualified as a nurse but was fired for sub-standard performance, got work as a psychiatric nurse and was fired for his bad attitude. Neither father nor mother wanted much to do with him, and he spent his twenties in and out of mental institutions. His mother committed suicide in 1970 after learning she had cancer, and Gary reportedly attempted the same act as many as thirteen times.

In 1971 he gave new meaning to the phrase 'living in a world of his own' – creating his own church, the United Church of the Ministers of God. There was only ever one minister – Bishop Heidnik – and the core members of his small congregation were mentally handicapped African-American women from a nearby

institution. Bingo and loan sharking paid the Bishop's salary, and the congregation fulfilled his sexual needs, often *en masse*. He used some of the money to play the stock exchange, and proved himself either smart or lucky – by 1977 he had accumulated over $35,000. He invested this with Merrill Lynch, and saw it rise to almost $500,000 over the next decade. Since his church was registered as a charity he paid virtually no tax.

Early in 1978 Heidnik's mentally handicapped girlfriend gave birth to his child, but nothing much changed in the

'Don't worry', he told the terrified woman – the hole was for punishment, not burial. And she would not be alone for long: the basement was big enough for ten women, and the plan was that each of them would bear him a child.

Bishop's lifestyle. In May he broke his girlfriend's sister out of a mental institution and hid her away in his basement. When police came looking for the woman, they found she had endured a regime of beatings and sexual abuse. Heidnik received a three-to-seven year sentence for unlawful imprisonment and deviant sex. During his time in the state penitentiary he again attempted suicide on several occasions, once by swallowing a lightbulb.

He re-emerged, aged forty, in April 1983. His child had been put in a home, but his material wealth had continued to grow in his absence, allowing him to purchase the property at 3520 North Marshall Street which would come to be known as the 'House of Horrors'. The group sex sessions with black women resumed, but Heidnik decided he also wanted a Filipino wife. A visit to a matrimonial agency and several plausible letters served one up. Betty Disto arrived, married him, and then discovered that she had to share a bed with his congregation. When she protested, he beat her. After three months of that, she fled.

It would appear that all these people running away from him was becoming really irritating. A plan began forming in his mind, a plan for a Heidnik Utopia, one world from which escape would not be possible. On 26 November 1986 he started to gather its population, picking up black prostitute Josefina Rivera and bringing her home. She thought she was being paid for a few minutes' sex, but found herself shackled to a sewerage pipe in Heidnik's basement, watching him digging a hole in the earth floor. 'Don't worry,' he told the terrified woman – the hole was for punishment, not burial. And she would not be alone for long: the basement was big enough for ten women, and the plan was that each of them would bear him a child. Later that day she managed to get the boards off a window and scream for help, but only Heidnik came. He beat her, threw her in the punishment hole, and left her with full volume rock music for twenty-seven hours.

Three days after abducting Rivera, he kidnapped an old girlfriend, Sandy Lindsay. Several years earlier she had aborted his baby, and Heidnik had neither forgotten nor forgiven. Through December the two women were kept in steadily deteriorating conditions. There were no washing or toilet facilities, and their initial diet of oatmeal and bread was soon

replaced by dog-food sandwiches. Both women were subject to daily beatings and rapes from Heidnik, and were often forced to beat each other. Real or imagined protests were punished by a spell in the earthen hole, crammed in a space only four feet square, under a plywood lid and its sandbag weight.

Between 22 December and 19 January Heidnik lured three more African-American women – Lisa Thomas, Deborah Dudley and Jacqueline Askins. The rapes and beatings continued, but the higher population encouraged a new command structure, and Heidnik elevated Josefina Rivera to 'trusty' status. In return for fewer punishments and the odd meal out, she helped him keep the others in order. She later claimed that she had no choice if she wanted to live, but some of the others thought she went further than she needed to.

Death

Towards the end of January, Sandy Lindsay was hung by the hands from the ceiling as a punishment for trying to escape. Heidnik left her there for a week, then seemed surprised when she died of exhaustion. Her death brought no

amelioration of his regime though. On the contrary, it grew harsher. Not long after Lindsay's body was taken upstairs, the house resounded to the whine of a power saw. And then a sickly smell drifted down to the basement, a smell the women soon recognized in their daily 'dog-food' sandwiches. Anxious to leave no doubt, Heidnik took Dudley upstairs and showed her Lindsay's severed head in a pot on the stove. They were being fed the rest of her, he said. He had apparently got the idea from the movie *Eating Raoul*.

On 18 February he experimented with a new type of punishment. He crammed all but Rivera in the hole, filled it with water, and used bare wires to give them electric shocks. Dudley died. Around the same time he pierced all but Rivera's eardrums with a screwdriver. He did not want them discussing any rescue attempt.

Rivera was with him when he buried Dudley in a New Jersey park on 22 March, and when he picked up his last victim, Agnes Adams, on the following day. On 24 March, Rivera warned him that Adams' family might go to the police if she simply disappeared; a single visit would set their minds at rest.

It worked. He left her at the corner

where, four months earlier, he had picked her up. Rivera went straight to the police, who were eventually convinced by the shackle-marks on her ankles. Investigating officers forced their way into 3520 North Marshall Street at 4.30 the following morning, arrested the startled Heidnik and brought an end to his prisoners' dreadful ordeal. In the fridge they found a human forearm and around 24 pounds of neatly packaged human meat.

The story soon got out, and Heidnik was beaten up by other prisoners within hours of his arrest. His father told reporters 'I hope to hell they hang him, and you can quote me on that. I'll even pull the rope.' He neglected to add how hard he had tried to infect both his sons with his own virulent racism. 'A black life,' he had apparently often told them, 'has no value' (see Marriner, Bibliography).

The defence plea of insanity was torpedoed by the judge's refusal to admit Heidnik's record of mental illness as evidence. With no other context for judgement, the jury went by the crimes and opted for death. After eleven years on Pennsylvania's death row, Heidnik was finally executed by lethal injection in July 1999.

Witnesses to Heidnik's execution, Tracey Lomax and Carolyn Johnson were sisters of two of his victims

The Genesee River killer

Arthur Shawcross was born in Watertown, New York on 6 June 1945, the first anniversary of D-Day. He had a less than happy childhood, but it seems that his parents – unlike the Kempers and Heidniks – were relatively blame-free. When Shawcross was finally put away for

life he claimed his mother had abused him, setting in motion an eager search for corroborative evidence. None has ever been found. He was a late talker, a chronic bed-wetter, and the butt of schoolmates' teasing, but it seems unlikely that he was physically abused.

Having struck out on 'nurture' – or the

lack of it being a reason for Shawcross' behaviour – the researchers moved on to 'nature'. Here they struck gold, not once but three times. Shawcross had suffered several severe head injuries, with lasting consequences for his frontal lobe. He was born with an extra Y chromosome, a condition said to generate violent antisocial behaviour. And his body contained ten times the normal load of kryptopyrrole chemicals, which are associated with extreme mood swings and violent rages.

Shawcross himself blamed his troubles – and those of his unfortunate victims – on the Vietnam War. Drafted in 1964, he certainly witnessed many incidents of atrocious brutality and sadism, but there is little sense that he was shocked by any of them. On the contrary, he seems to have revelled in the blood and cruelty. He described one encounter with two Vietnamese women – in which he killed and ate the roasted flesh of one before raping and killing the other – with the sort of deadpan relish that sent a shiver down the spines of those hearing his testimony.

Life must have seemed tame when he came back home. He took to beating his Christian Scientist second wife, who went to consult a psychiatrist about him. The

In the fridge they found a human forearm and around 24 pounds of neatly packaged human meat. The story soon got out and Heidnik was beaten up by other prisoners within hours of his arrest.

Shawcross on his first arrest. Prison proved no deterrent

> He pretended to take a great interest in his own case. Like Peter Kurten, he warned his wife – in Shawcross' case, his mistress as well – to take precautions against himself.

psychiatrist recommended commital and therapy, but she thought he was exaggerating the problem, and refused to sign the papers. Two years later her husband killed two children, eight-year-old Karen Hill and ten-year-old Jack Blake. Arrested and convicted for raping and killing the girl, he was given a twenty-five year sentence. In prison he confessed to the boy's murder, but not, apparently, until the body had decomposed, because he later claimed to have eaten the heart and genitals.

He was released after only fifteen years. Two communities refused to have him before he settled, unnoticed, in Rochester, New York. He found a third wife and a mistress, and soon started killing again. Between February 1988 and January 1990 Shawcross murdered eleven women, nine of them prostitutes. After strangling or beating them to death, he mutilated their bodies, a process which gave him great sexual satisfaction. In two cases he cut up their bodies and ate parts.

He pretended to take a great interest in his own case. Like Peter Kurten, he warned his wife – in Shawcross' case, his mistress as well – to take precautions against himself. Like Fritz Haarmann and Ed Kemper he hung around in coffee bars, talking to the police whenever he could.

The police were at a complete loss. No one, it seems, went to the trouble of checking out which convicted sex-murderers were on parole in the area. In the event, it was only a ludicrous piece of luck which led to Shawcross' capture – he was spotting by a police helicopter urinating off a bridge, with a body visible in the river below.

His first arrest proved abortive, however, – he did not fit the police profile. It was only when they found one of the dead women's earrings in his car that he was arrested again, and questioned until he broke. Shawcross confessed to eleven killings, including two the police were unaware of. He told them about his cannibalism, and how he had often returned to the decomposing bodies for a sexual recharge. Most of the physical evidence was inconclusive, and a few of the psychiatrists were unconvinced, but most believed Shawcross was what he claimed to be – a cannibal-killer. The real arguments came later, over why. Shawcross, meanwhile, was serving the first of ten consecutive twenty-five year sentences. He seems likely to die in prison.

The face of an incorrigible killer: Shawcross was in and out of prison for a string of horrific crimes

Stanley Dean Baker

It would be nice to report that cannibal-killers have grown rarer as humanity advances, but it seems more likely that they are growing more common. This is no great surprise – great swathes of our culture now demonstrate the lack of connective emotion which once seemed the preserve of the individual. Societies with growing problems breed people with growing problems.

'I have a problem'

One such, as he freely admitted, was Stanley Dean Baker. His one (and so far as we know, only) victim was dragged out of

Given that it was such an extreme crime, it seems unlikely that James Schlosser was Stanley Dean Baker's only victim

> **Once the other man was asleep, he had shot him through the head with a .22 pistol and cut up the body. He had eaten the heart raw and taken a couple of fingers for something to chew on.**

the Yellowstone River on 11 July 1970. The arms had been chopped off at the shoulders, the legs at the knees. The head was missing, and so, the attending doctor soon realized, was the heart. The police were resigned to a long wait for identification, but struck lucky within thirty-six hours. A young man matching the age and size of the victim had already been reported missing from a nearby town, and had been heading for the area in question in his yellow sports car. His name was James Schlosser.

The police had only just put out a description of the yellow sports car when it ran into a truck, several hundred miles away in California. The car was a write-off, so the truck's owner offered to take the car's driver and passenger – two tall hippies with long hair – to the next available phone to report the accident. They accepted readily – a lift was a lift – but promptly ran off when he stopped at a service station. The truck owner phoned the police himself, and passed on the sports car's registration number. The

requisite bells went off, and the California Highway Patrol was asked to keep a lookout for the two hippies.

They were picked up a few miles away, still hitching their way down the road to nowhere. The two men were searched. The blonder of the two, whose name was Stanley Dean Baker, had the *Satanic Bible* in his bag and what looked like chicken bones in his pocket. But they were not. 'They're human fingers,' Baker told the cops. 'I have a problem – I'm a cannibal' (see Marriner, Bibliography).

He had hitched a lift with Schlosser in the two-seater, leaving his companion behind. When Schlosser said he was going camping in Yellowstone National Park, Baker had tagged along. Once the other man was asleep, he had shot him through the head with a .22 pistol and cut up the body. He had eaten the heart raw and taken a couple of fingers for something to chew on.

The 'Chicago Rippers'

Baker's career as a cannibal-murderer was free of sadism and mercifully brief. Would that the same could be said of the 'Chicago Rippers' – Robin Gecht, Ed Spreitzer, Andrew and Thomas Kokoraleis. This gang of twisted young men mutilated and killed as many as eighteen women between September 1981 and October 1982.

Their leader, the 30-year-old Gecht, combined an interest in satanism with a breast fixation, and devised a killing ritual to satisfy both. Women were taken back to Gecht's 'Satanic Chapel', where they were raped and tortured. Their left breasts were sliced off with a wire garotte, and eaten. The remains were kept in a trophy box. At some point in the process the victims would die.

That any individual could devise and practise such a ritual seems adequate cause for horror. That Chicago could boast as many as four young Americans willing to wallow in such sadism seems cause for despair. At least they were finally caught, when one of the victims they left for dead proved otherwise and was able to testify against them. All but Gecht confessed, but only Andrew Kokoraleis was executed.

Tales of Manhattan

New York City has had more than its share of serial killers, but only two well-known cannibal-killers since Albert Fish. History teacher Albert Fentress briefly hit the headlines in 1979 when he shot, dissected and ate one of his students. He was locked away in a mental institution. Ten years later, rumour of another cannibal feast began spreading around the drug-friendly Tompkins Square area of East Side Manhattan. An exotic dancer named Monica Beerle had disappeared, and someone had seen her head in a pot. A friend approached a policeman working

Daniel Rakowitz: a studied image that went too far?

on another case, and convinced him there was more to the story than drug-induced visions. He tracked down the original witness, who put him on to Monica's boyfriend, the 'scary' Daniel Rakowitz. Rakowitz was a 28-year-old Texan with a beard and a penchant for wearing dead chickens around his neck. Further

> **'Her left leg was undamaged, so I took out a knife and cut off her calf, just the muscle. I brought it to the house, washed it, skinned it, and that night I made myself some patties...'**

investigation revealed that he had emptied Monica's flat before moving on, and had told one of her friends that he had killed her. 'I did not mean it, but I killed her', he said, before corroborating the original witness report. 'It got out of hand. I killed her and boiled her head. Then I made soup of her brains. It tasted pretty good' (see Marriner, Bibliography). When arrested, Rakowitz calmly told police what had happened, and where they could find Monica's bones – in the undignified resting place of a plastic bucket at the Port Authority left luggage.

A 'wild idea'

The last Gein disciple had the usual sad catalogue of childhood woes – dressing in his grandmother's clothes at five, reading bondage magazines at ten, and a developing interest in witchcraft and Satanism through his teens. John Weber was good at hiding his urge towards sexual sadism, however, and when his seventeen-year-old sister-in-law Carla suddenly disappeared he was quickly dismissed as a possible suspect.

Twenty-two months later he phoned the police to report a violent attack on his wife. Two men had abducted her, he said. They had stabbed her in several places and

beaten her badly around the head, but she was alive. He had spent the day tending to her wounds, or he would have called them earlier.

Taped confession

Once out of his reach in hospital, his wife told the police what had really happened. Her husband had driven her out into the countryside and forced her to write several letters and cheques. After raping her, he had repeatedly struck her across the face with a shovel, before suddenly breaking down and begging her forgiveness. During the attack he had threatened to make her 'disappear like Carla disappeared.'

The police searched Weber's car and found a taped confession of how he had tortured, raped and mutilated Carla before choking her to death. And then, he said, 'I had this wild idea. Her left leg was undamaged, so I took out a knife and cut off her calf, just the muscle. I brought it to the house, washed it, skinned it, and that night I made myself some patties from Carla's leg.' Later he cooked the girl's breast. 'And you know, human meat does not taste that bad,' he told the tape. 'I was surprised. Actually it tasted good' (see Marriner, Bibliography).

Jeffrey Dahmer

Jeffrey Dahmer's childhood in Bath, Ohio offered a few clues to his future notoriety, but nothing too obvious. His parents rowed a lot but they stayed together, albeit at the cost of his mother developing an addiction to painkillers. The boy had what seemed an unhealthy interest in dissecting road kill, but kept his sadistic games with live animals to himself. Lionel Dahmer hoped that his son's hobby would lead to a career in anatomical science, and was only just off the mark – he would certainly make use of the knowledge gained. Jeffrey's schoolmates knew something was wrong – his sense of humour was 'cruel and really dark', and he was 'weird, so emotionless' (see Marriner, Bibliography).

Dahmer was thirteen when he realized he was gay, and never seems to have come to terms with the fact. His father, a strict Lutheran, considered homosexuality a sin, and Dahmer seems to have agreed with him. Almost from the beginning, his gayness was entangled with necrophiliac fantasies. Later, when he was living what passed for a normal gay life in Milwaukee, he would still confide to a straight friends that he hated his fellow-gays.

As an angst-ridden teenager, he began

He took a storefront mannequin home to bed, fantasized about grave-robbing, and finally gave in – throwing himself into Milwaukee's gay scene.

One of the most notorious US criminals, Jeffrey Dahmer had a prodigious appetite for killing – and for human flesh

drinking heavily, and in the summer of 1978 – a month before his parents finally divorced – he committed his first murder. It was not premeditated. Dahmer picked up Steven Hicks, an eighteen year-old hitchhiker he fancied, and asked him back for a drink, a toke and maybe something more. A few hours later the man wanted to leave but Dahmer did not want him to go, so he caved in his skull with a barbell. Next morning he solved the problem of what to do with the body by cutting it up and stuffing the pieces into three large garbage bags, but only after he had slit open the stomach and had a good look inside. He was eighteen years old.

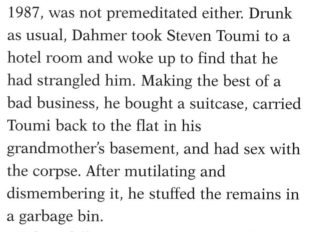

A few hours later the man wanted to leave but Dahmer did not want him to go, so he caved in his skull with a barbell.

Learning the ropes

How this first murder affected Dahmer is hard to judge. It seems probable that he went nine years before killing again, which suggests a certain level of self-restraint. His drinking got worse, restricting his time at university to one term and bringing down the curtain on a two-year career in the army. He went back to live with his father, who found the drinking too much and moved him on to his grandmother in Wisconsin. After a couple of arrests for exposing himself in public, Dahmer tried religion, joining his grandmother in bible reading and churchgoing. It worked for a while, but the old urges wouldn't let him be. He took a storefront mannequin home to bed, fantasized about grave-robbing, and finally gave in – throwing himself into Milwaukee's flourishing gay bathhouse scene. He soon realized that he preferred his partners unconscious, and took to drugging them. Word seeped out, and the bathhouses began revoking his membership.

His second killing, on 16 November 1987, was not premeditated either. Drunk as usual, Dahmer took Steven Toumi to a hotel room and woke up to find that he had strangled him. Making the best of a bad business, he bought a suitcase, carried Toumi back to the flat in his grandmother's basement, and had sex with the corpse. After mutilating and dismembering it, he stuffed the remains in a garbage bin.

Others followed: a fourteen year-old Native American named James Doxtator was next, then Richard Guerrero, a twenty-five-year-old Mexican. Dahmer, unusually for a serial killer, was not choosy about race. He hadn't yet taken to

Next morning he solved the problem of what to do with the body by cutting it up and stuffing the pieces into three large garbage bags...

keeping souvenirs of his victims, but the dismemberments were making the place smell like an abattoir. This and other problems associated with his drinking encouraged his grandmother to give him his marching orders in the summer of

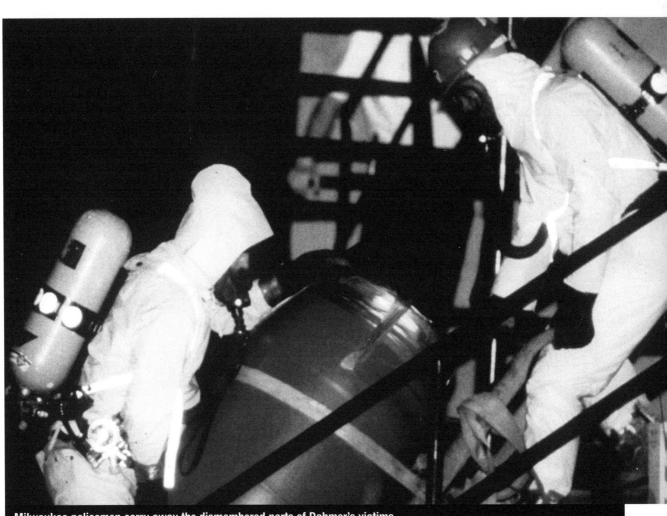

Milwaukee policemen carry away the dismembered parts of Dahmer's victims

1988. He rented an apartment in Milwaukee and invited one thirteen-year-old boy to the house-warming. He misjudged the drug dose for once, the boy went home, and his parents contacted the police. Dahmer almost talked himself out of it, but ended up spending ten months in a corrective detention facility.

Killing spree

In June 1990 he moved back into the apartment. Over the next thirteen months Dahmer murdered twelve young males, usually by drugging and strangling them. Necrophiliac sex and dissection would follow, but he no longer felt the need to throw the pieces away. Some body parts were frozen and neatly packed in polythene, others were preserved in jars of formaldehyde. Like Ed Kemper, he recorded each step of the process with a trusty polaroid camera, filling albums with the resulting snaps.

Dahmer enjoyed masturbating in front of severed heads, particularly one which he had painted grey to look like a medical model. He also painted one penis, and kept several others in jars. Those bits he did not want were dissolved in acid and flushed down the toilet. Most bizarre of all, he

'It started out as experimentation, because it made me feel like they were part of me.'

harboured an ambition to create the perfect sex slave, and experimented with an electric drill on his unconscious victims, dribbling acid into what he thought were appropriate areas of their brains.

Dahmer's cannibalism seems to have been something of an afterthought. He could not quite remember when it started,

Over the next thirteen months Dahmer murdered twelve young males, usually by drugging and strangling them...dissection would follow, but he no longer felt the need to throw the [body parts] away.

but thought it was probably with his sixth or seventh victim. 'It started out as experimentation, because it made me feel like they were more part of me' (see Korn, Radice and Hawes, Bibliography). He had eaten livers, hearts, thighs and biceps from three of his victims. The biceps had been tastiest, like 'filet mignon'. He had ground some of the flesh into patties and experimented with seasonings.

He was almost caught in May 1991 when a fourteen year-old victim escaped from his apartment and managed to reach a group of police officers in the street. The boy was naked and bleeding, but the drugs had made him incoherent, and Dahmer persuaded the hapless cops to hand him back. Two months later another would-be victim's escape attempt proved more successful. This time the cops took care to look round the apartment, and the polaroids of sex with severed heads were a bit of a giveaway. Dahmer was arrested, and his apartment searched from top to bottom.

Those who did the searching were later treated to counselling as what they found was a roll-call of the truly gruesome: a seven gallon drum containing three torsos in varying states of decomposition, zip-locked bags of human flesh, a freezer full of heads, a collection of dried genitals and a complete skeleton.

Confronted with all this, his trial jury decided he was sane. It seemed a strange message to send, but Dahmer was too busy getting religion to notice. Sentenced to fifteen consecutive life terms – an unlikely 1,070 years – he refused the protection of solitary confinement and was clubbed to death by a fellow prisoner. The weapon at least was familiar – it was a barbell.

Stalin's children

'The Rostov Ripper'

The most prolific cannibal-killer of modern times was born, appropriately enough, in famine-stricken 1930s Ukraine. Andrei Chikatilo's childhood featured all the usual symptoms and a few more besides. When Andrei was four, his mother told him that his older brother Stepan had been taken away and eaten, and then abused him for wetting the bed. His father, like the rest of the country, was soon at war. Captured by the Germans, he eventually came home to Stalin's version of the hero's welcome – several years in an Arctic labour camp. The family was sent to the Soviet equivalent of Coventry.

Andrei came through it all physically intact, but something had definitely gone awry in his emotional and sexual wiring. His experiences with girls brought ejaculations but no erections, so he tried to avoid them, concentrating on his studies and his Party work in the Donbass mining region. His sister played Cupid, introducing him to her friend Feodosiya, a miner's daughter. Chikatilo had no obvious vices – he did not drink, smoke or shout his own praises – and Feodosiya decided she could

do a lot worse. They married in 1963.

His sexual problems soon became apparent, but they still managed to have two children; Ludmilla in 1965 and Yuri in 1969. Feodosiya had no complaints – her husband worked hard at his job as a teacher, and was kind to her and their children.

Other people's children were another matter. Chikatilo was caught molesting some of his pupils, and in 1978 he was quietly transferred to a less sensitive job at a mining school in Shakhty. He continued writing articles on patriotism and Soviet morality for the local Party press, and took

Chikatilo: charged with killing and mutilating fifty-two boys, girls and women over twelve years

more care with his illicit sex life. Unbeknown to his wife, he rented a shack on the other side of town, where he 'entertained' both willing prostitutes and unwilling young girls. He took care not to go too far with the latter, and seems, for several months, to have managed some sort of bargain with the devils inside him.

Then, in December of that year, it all fell apart. He met nine year-old Lena Zakotnova at a tram stop, and struck up a conversation. She was hopping from foot to foot, and confided to the fatherly Chikatilo that she badly needed a toilet. He lived just round the corner, he said. She could use his. Once he had her at his mercy, Chikatilo

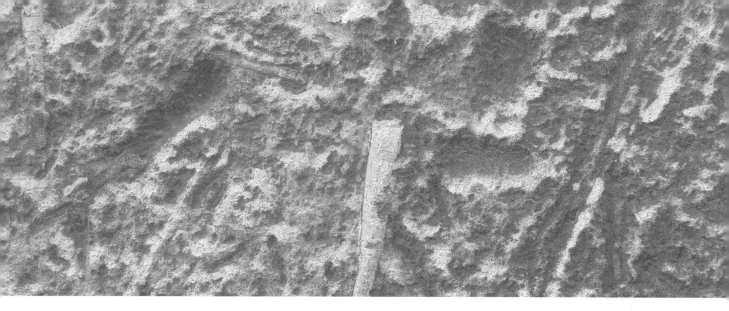

tried and failed to rape the young girl. On impulse, he picked up a sharp knife, stabbing her repeatedly in what was all too obviously a sexual frenzy. Finally, at the age of forty-two, he had found what he needed.

He was almost caught. The body was recovered from the river, and people had seen him with the girl. His wife, however, swore he had been at home with her, and

Unbeknown to his wife, he rented a shack on the other side of town, where he 'entertained' both willing prostitutes and unwilling girls.

the police soon found a better scapegoat – a man named Kravchenko, who had a record of similar crimes and lived just around the corner. Certain of their man, the police were not fussy about how they got their confession. Kravchenko was executed in 1983, still protesting his innocence.

By that time Chikatilo was almost into double figures. It took him almost three years to kill again, but the second murder, when it eventually came, marked another

giant step beyond human restraint. Seventeen year-old runaway Larisa Tkachenko agreed to paid sex, but never came back from their walk in the woods outside Rostov. Chikatilo half strangled the girl before biting her neck and drinking her blood, and then went to work with his knife. Offended by the sight of her naked, mutilated body, he covered it up with copies of *Pravda* and *Young Communist*.

Earlier that year he had quit teaching for a job managing supplies for a construction firm. This new work afforded him a licence to travel, and he made full use of it, murdering at least fifty-one women and children over the next nine years. Chikatilo was good at talking to strangers, and particularly good at getting children to trust him. 'He had an amazing talent for it', one of the investigating officers said later. 'He could join a bus queue and say to the person in front: "Hey, where did you buy those beautiful mushrooms?", and before you knew it he would have the whole crowd chatting' (see Martingale, Bibliography).

After killing his third victim, Lyuba Biryuk, in June 1982, all restraint seemed to vanish. He killed six times in the next six months, and with ever-increasing ferocity. He abandoned his exclusive

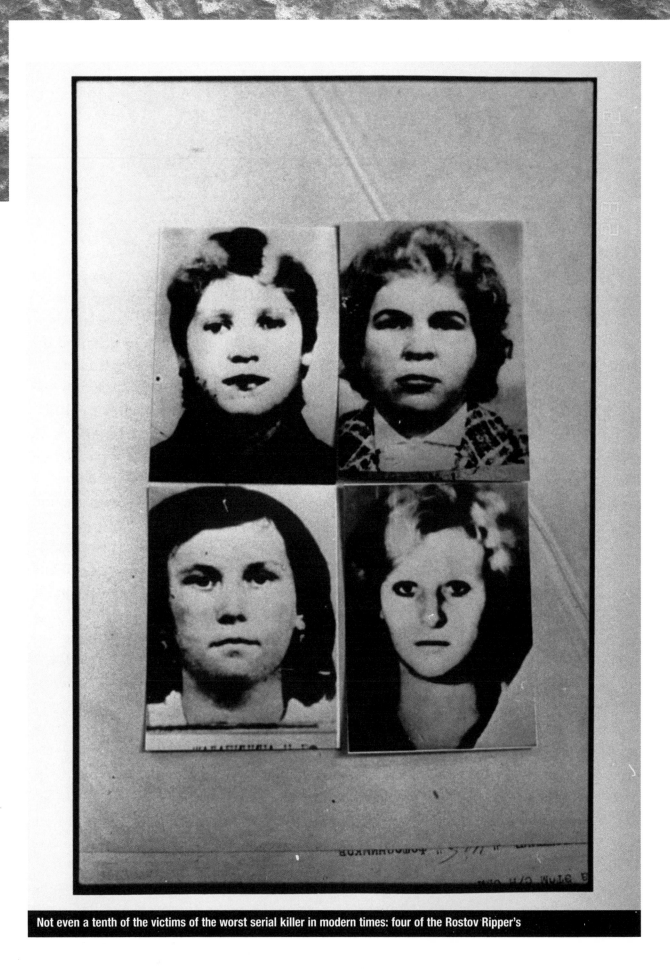

Not even a tenth of the victims of the worst serial killer in modern times: four of the Rostov Ripper's

concentration on girls; boys offered new possibilities for his knife and, as a bonus, more confusion for the police. He began stabbing out eyes as a matter of course, and gouged several from their sockets. Tongues, noses, lips, breasts and genitals were all sliced off; scrotums emptied of their testes. And there was increasing evidence that he was eating the parts he removed – traces of fires were often found near the bodies. His wife later testified that he took pots and pans on his trips away from home.

The wounds were often shallower than before, as if he was trying to string out the pain before death. Most cannibal-killers do their killing first, and spare their victims the horrors that follow. For Chikatilo, the horror was the point.

In 1984 he was arrested for stealing three rolls of linoleum, and kicked out of the Party. He responded by killing ten people in two months. In this same year police officers saw him acting suspiciously on one occasion, and watched for nine hours while he made repeated attempts to pick up strangers. Eventually they took him in. His briefcase contained an eight-inch knife and some rope, which looked extremely suspicious. But his blood group failed to match the semen found on the Ripper's victims, so they had to let him go. By the end of 1984 his personal death toll had risen beyond thirty.

A team from the Soviet Union's Department for Crimes of Special Importance was sent down to the Donbass. Over the next few years it carried out an investigation of such staggering thoroughness that ninety-five unsolved murder cases were cleared up.

He was charged with thirty-six murders and confessed to another nineteen. Questioned for eighteen months by police and psychiatrists, he showed a remarkable memory for each of his victims.

Chikatilo's, however, were not among them. The killings went on, particularly in the region around Rostov. The police saturated the surrounding countryside, until almost everyone at large was a cop in disguise. And finally, in November 1990, they got their breakthrough. Chikatilo was stopped and questioned when a cop saw him emerge from the forest and stop to

wash his hands and shoes at a hydrant. He answered the queries convincingly enough, but back at headquarters his name rang a bell with the officer in charge of the hunt. Issa Kostoyev looked at Chikatilo's file, and remembered something else he had recently read, that blood and semen types were not always identical. His men searched the area where Chikatilo had been seen, and found another body.

Chikatilo was watched for a while, but the risk of him killing again seemed too great, and he was finally arrested. This time his semen was tested, and proved a match. He was charged with thirty-six murders, and promptly confessed to another nineteen. Questioned for eighteen months by police and psychiatrists, he showed a remarkable memory for each of his victims.

The trial was a circus. A cage was built in the courthouse, partly to keep Chikatilo in, mostly to keep the victims' relatives out. He started out lucidly, arguing that the judges had already decided his guilt, but eventually opted for feigning insanity, singing the *Internationale* and waving his penis at the audience. The court decided he was sane, and sentenced him to death. In February 1994 he was given the classic Stalinist execution – a trip to the cellar for a bullet in the back of the head.

Freedom's menu

Just as survival cannibalism flourished in the Soviet Union's traumatic early decades, so a different kind of cannibalism has flourished in the opening years of its

capitalist successors. No one has come close to matching Chikatilo's murder roll, but an epidemic of opportunistic cannibalism seems to have broken out in the post-Soviet world. Neither communism nor capitalism seems clear of blame – the one nurtured these cannibals from birth, the other supplied the chaos and shortages which they exploited.

Only Nikolai Dzhumagaliev warrants inclusion among the cannibal serial killers. This smartly-dressed 'perfect gentleman'

Nikolai 'Metal Fang' Dzhumagaliev (second from left) stands handcuffed to Colonel Yuri Dubyagin, Chief of the Moscow Police

with stainless steel teeth – the police called him 'Metal Fang' – raped, dismembered and partly ate an unknown number of women in ex-Soviet Central Asia in the 1990s. The facts of his case are hard to pin down – different reports place him in Uzbekistan, Kazakhstan and Kyrgyzstan – but it seems likely that his victims were numerous, and that he made a habit of serving human flesh to unsuspecting guests. Since his capture and conviction,

he has twice escaped from mental institutions, but is thankfully, for the present, behind bars.

Alexander Zapantsiev, a citizen of the Ural industrial town of Chelyabinsk, was much more typical. The town's main claim to fame was a major nuclear accident, and the Soviet Union's expiration left it awash with unemployment, alcoholism and cynicism. One particular evening Zapantsiev and his drinking partner

Valdemar Suzik had a blazing row, and the latter ended up dead. He cut up the corpse to ease the problem of disposal, and hosted a new year's feast with some of his fellow-residents, telling them that the strange-tasting meat was veal, a gift from a butcher friend. He sold more of Suzik at the market, and kept the rest in his fridge.

When Suzik was reported missing, the witness trail led straight to Zapantsiev. Under questioning, he claimed that Suzik's death had been an accident, that his head had hit the oven as he fell. He admitted to dismembering the body and hiding the parts, and told the police where to dig them up. In doing so, they unearthed a new question – where was the flesh? The inspector in charge suddenly remembered his first visit to Zapantsiev's apartment, and the fridge full of 'dog meat'.

A similar story unfolded in Manturovo, a small dead-end town north-east of

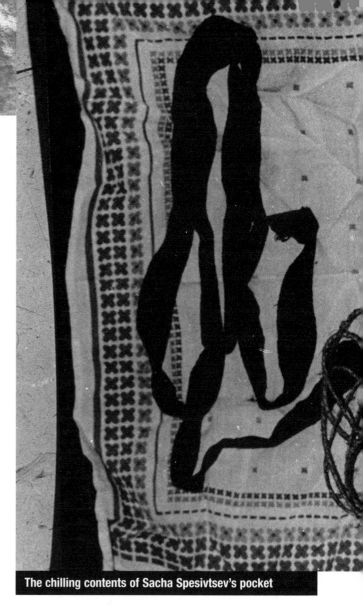
The chilling contents of Sacha Spesivtsev's pocket

He murdered three visitors in succession, marinading their flesh in plastic bags, storing their blood in Pepsi bottles and hanging their severed ears on his wall for wintertime snacks.

Moscow. In this case, however, there was no slim chance of accidental death. Vitaly Bezrodnov and his girlfriend Valentina Dolbilina carefully weighed up the meat on their two comatose drinking companions before decapitating the chosen one with an axe. Soon fifteen pounds of flesh had been carved from the corpse and the smell of cooking was wafting through the block. It attracted one of the neighbours, who picked some frying flesh from the pan and popped it in his mouth, unaware he was eating his brother. When questioned about her cannibalism, Dolbilina said she had been depressed.

Zapantsiev, Bezrodnov and Dolbilina were all sent to prison, where the newspapers claimed that cannibalism was rife. Four men sharing a cell in Semipalatinsk Prison decided they must be missing out, and vowed to eat their next cell mate. They cooked some of him on a hotplate and boiled some in their electric kettle. Andrei Maslich, a prisoner in the

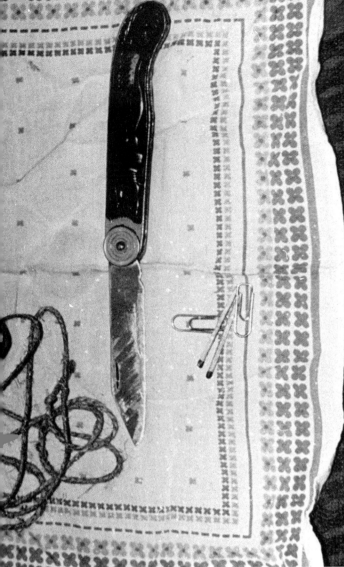

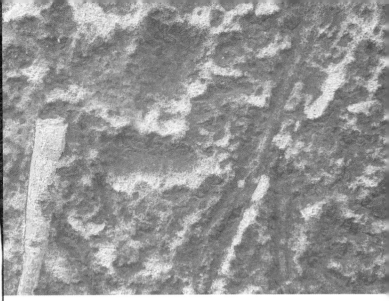

Siberian town of Barnaul, showed even more ingenuity. He strangled his cell mate, cut out his liver with a shard of glass, and popped it in a mug of water. He then made a fire from his bedding, boiled the liver into soup, and drank it.

The list goes on. Three men and a woman in Zhitomir were arrested for the killing and consumption of six others in a satanic ritual. An ex-convict in the Crimea is documented as eating three people, while a man in Kemerovo killed a friend because he needed filling for his ravioli. In Berezniki two market traders killed a third in a drunken row, ate what they could and sold the rest.

All a bit small-time, you might think, hardly worth mentioning in the company of a monster like Chikatilo. Vladimir Nikolayev was a little more ambitious – the police found pans of human flesh cooking on his stove when they went to arrest him, and there were other bodies in the larder of snow on his balcony. Ilshat Kuzikov was perhaps a little too crazy to take seriously, unless you were one of his victims. He murdered three visitors in succession, marinating their flesh in plastic bags, storing their blood in Pepsi bottles, and hanging their severed ears on his wall for wintertime snacks. Sacha Spesivtsev might have been a contender, but lacked the intelligence. He had evil to spare, and would have loved Chikatilo's politics. He grew up in the Siberian coal town of Novokuznetsk, learned from his father how to abuse women, and embarked on a Chikatilo-meets-Vlad-the-Impaler-style crusade to clear the streets of the undeserving poor. Spesivtsev was caught when a plumber broke into his flat to stem a leak, and found he had stumbled into an abattoir. By this time the twenty-seven-year-old Spesivtsev and his trusty Dobermann had killed and eaten around nineteen girls. Sentenced to death, he made the most of the time that was left to him, writing poems about the evils of democracy.

A German revival

'The Ruhr Hunter'

Joachim Kroll was born in April 1933, three months after Hitler came to power. His father was sent, like so many before him, into a war with the Soviet Union from which he never returned. In 1947 the rest of the family escaped from the Soviet-occupied zone and settled in the Ruhr, Germany's main industrial area.

Joachim had only had a few years of schooling, and was considered slow enough to warrant a mentally-handicapped label. His four siblings had all left home when his mother died in 1955, leaving him to fend for himself, both economically and emotionally. Less than three weeks later, he killed for the first time. In a village north of the Ruhr he seized and strangled nineteen year-old Irmgard Strehl, before stripping, raping and cutting her open. It was the beginning of a murder spree lasting more than twenty years.

For someone supposedly slow on the uptake, Kroll demonstrated, time and time again, a keen awareness of how not to get caught. He eventually confessed to fourteen murders, but was quite prepared to concede that he had probably forgotten a few, and some of the longer gaps between victims do seem unlikely. Given that all his murders were committed in the same part of the country, it seems incredible that he never left an obvious clue to his identity.

All Kroll's victims but one were female (the single male was only killed to get at his girlfriend), but their ages ranged from four to sixty-one. Almost all were strangled first, but only some were cut up for meat. He later told police that his cannibalism was just a way of saving on his shopping bill, and that even then he only took flesh that looked really tender. At the time his selectivity had the

Hardly the face of a killer: Kroll went on a killing spree that lasted more than twenty years

unwitting bonus of confusing the authorities. And confuse them it did, with tragic consequences. Three men committed suicide after being falsely accused of Kroll's crimes.

His capture in 1976 demonstrated either lack of intelligence or a desire to be caught. After murdering and butchering four-year-old Monika Kettner, he warned a fellow-tenant that their shared toilet was

For someone supposedly slow on the uptake, Kroll demonstrated, time and time again, a keen awareness of how not to get caught.

blocked with 'guts'. The fellow-tenant had a look, did not like what he saw, and went for the police. They found a complete set of child-size organs obstructing the pipe.

In Kroll's flat they found other remains – pieces of raw flesh in the fridge, wrapped body parts in the freezer and, most disturbing of all, a stew bubbling on the hob that contained carrots, potatoes and a tiny hand. In the bedroom an inflatable rubber sex doll was primed for action. He used to strangle it while he masturbated, Kroll told the cops. After his arrest he

asked for the operation which would make him harmless to women, and expressed the hope that he would be home in time for supper. He died of a heart attack fifteen years later, still serving the first of nine consecutive life sentences.

Woman cannibal

Anna Zimmerman was also keen to save on her butcher's bill, but in most other respects she remains something of a mystery. Female cannibal-killers are a rare species, and reading her story there is little sense of any compulsion at work. It seems more a case of why not – the opportunity presented itself, and she took it.

As far as the Mönchen Gladbach police were concerned, the story began with a missing barber, thirty-four year-old Josef Wirtz. His rent was due on Friday 1 June, and by the following Monday his landlord was beginning to suspect that Wirtz had skipped town. Finding that his tenant's clothes and possessions were still in the apartment, the landlord waited a few more days, and then went to the police. They agreed that the circumstances looked suspicious, and circulated a photo of Wirtz.

No sightings were reported, but almost five weeks later a woman walking in a park tripped on something half buried in the ground. It had been a head, but was not yet a skull. Four plastic bags full of bones were found nearby. A forensic team confirmed that the parts had once belonged to Wirtz, and offered the

...a woman walking in the park tripped on something half buried in the ground. It had been a head, but was not yet a skull. Four plastic bags full of bones were found nearby.

additional information that the bones had been stripped of flesh with a sharp butcher's knife: cannibalism seemed the only logical explanation.

Two of the plastic bags came from a video rental business, and detectives started checking out all the clients who had rented horror movies. Eventually they found themselves in Anna Zimmerman's flat. The large spiders and snakes on the floor were one clue, the butchered remains of a family pet on the kitchen table another. Questioned, Zimmerman denied knowing any Josef Wirtz, but then let slip that she knew he was a barber. A search of her flat revealed over fifty cartons containing human flesh, including one containing a penis.

She still proclaimed her innocence, but her estranged husband Wilhelm confessed to supplying the power saw used in the butchery. He said Wirtz had been Anna's lover for a couple of years, that she had

drugged him, tried and failed strangulation, and finally drowned him in the bath. She had used the power saw to cut him up on the kitchen table while he and the two kids sat in the next room. Wilhelm seemed unclear about motive, but thought sexual inadequacy might have had something to do with it.

'I am your flesh!'

Armin Meiwes was born in 1962. His parents owned a rambling manor house outside Rotenburg in central Germany, and it was here that he grew up, lived his adult life, and committed the acts for which he is now notorious.

His father, who left when Meiwes was only eight, had ignored him when he was still around. The boy's mother, on the other hand, was incapable of letting him alone, and her suffocating attentions made him an object of ridicule at school. Not surprisingly, Meiwes retreated into a fantasy world, inventing an imaginary brother named Franky. His plans for this brother, however, did not include the usual brotherly relations. Meiwes dreamt of binding Franky to himself in perpetuity by the simple act of consuming him. This fantasy, he told a packed courtroom years later, had developed in the years after his father's departure. 'And in the end I fulfilled it,' he concluded.

In 1981 Meiwes joined the army, but he continued to live at home, and took his mother with him on troop outings. At the end of the 1980s she became bed-ridden, and he left the army to train as a computer technician and look after her.

Brandes: what was his motivation for eating himself? A surreal question that will hopefully never be answered

Her death in 1999 set him free to pursue his fantasy. Hoping for like-minded guests, he set about renovating the rather dilapidated family home. Included in the make-over was a new 'slaughter room', complete with cage, meat-hook and pulley. By day he went to work, by night he trawled the internet for others who shared his cannibalistic fantasies. He spoke to more than two hundred of them on chatlines, and several came to visit after he posted the ad: 'Gay male seeks hunks 18–30 to slaughter.' Some allowed him to hoist them up on the hook and mark up the choicest cuts on their bodies with a

pen. None, however, was actually willing to be eaten.

Towards the end of 2000, a 43 year-old microchip engineer named Bernd-Jurgen Brandes replied to Meiwes' advertisement using the pseudonym 'Cator', and over the next few months they communicated by email. Brandes said he was willing to fill the role Meiwes had marked out for Franky. 'There is absolutely no way back for me,' he wrote, 'only forwards, through your teeth' (see Article 3, Bibliography).

In March 2001 Brandes wrote a will leaving everything to his unknowing gay partner, had it notarized, and took the

The smile, and teeth, of a convicted cannibal

After Brandes had consumed twenty sleeping tablets and half a bottle of schnapps to dull the expected pain, Meiwes removed his new friend's penis and testicles with a kitchen knife.

train westwards. According to Meiwes, Brandes met him at the station with the words: 'I am your Cator, I am your flesh' (see Anon, Bibliography).

Back at the house, they stripped off and discussed what they were about to do. After Brandes had consumed twenty sleeping tablets and half a bottle of schnapps to dull the expected pain, Meiwes removed his new friend's penis and testicles with a kitchen knife. This, like everything else which happened that evening, was faithfully recorded on his camcorder.

He then put the genitalia into the frying pan, and opened a bottle of white wine. The two men then ate as much of the sautéed flesh as they could manage, washing it down with the wine. By this time Brandes was losing a lot of blood, and Meiwes suggested that he take a bath. While Brandes bled out in the tub, Meiwes read part of a *Star Trek* novel and watched a Disney film on TV. 'It took so terribly long' he said at his trial.

Eventually a close-to-unconscious Brandes gave Meiwes permission to hang him up and finish him off. Meiwes did so, stabbing him several times. He then cut the fresh corpse into meal-size portions and stacked them – neatly wrapped and labelled – in his freezer. Parts like the head, which he considered inedible, were buried in the back garden. He then slowly worked his way through the frozen portions, cooking them with olive oil and garlic.

Meiwes would probably never have been caught if he had not tried to relive the experience. A new internet advertisement was reported to the police, who turned up at his door, searched the house, and found what was left of Brandes in the freezer and garden. Meiwes was only too willing to admit the killing and the eating. Both had been at the victim's request, he told the authorities, and he had the video evidence to prove it. Since cannibalism is not illegal in Germany, he was not charged with it, and Brandes' clear connivance in his own death made a conviction for murder unlikely. In 2004 Meiwes was convicted of manslaughter, and is currently serving an eight and a half-year sentence.

6: The Fascination With Cannibalism

Globalization

So far, almost all the modern cannibal-killers to stain these pages have been Germans, Americans or people who grew up in the old Soviet Union. Can cannibal-killers be a curse of superpowerdom? It does not seem likely, and nor does the notion that societies blessed with material success are more likely to throw up cruel and destructive weirdos. The Germany of the 1920s and the Russia of the 1980s were hardly overflowing with consumer luxuries.

It does seem possible that developed societies offer greater anonymity to commit such crimes – Third World shanty towns are generally lacking in closed doors to hide behind. But that does not explain the apparent lack of cannibal-killer cases in, say, Italy or Norway.

Of course, the developed world's quasi-monopoly could simply reflect the traditional limits of developed world news-gathering. Third World countries might have cannibal-killers in similar numbers, notorious in their own back yards but unseen blips on the international radar. If so, their time is coming. As news-gathering follows the globalizing trend, so any Dahmers and Chikatilos of the Third

Birds of a feather: Beverley Allitt was convicted in 1991 of the murder of four children and the attempted murder of nine others. Despite both being in prison, she was Mark Heggie's girlfriend for some time in the early 1990s

World will get to bask in a globalized spotlight. Where cannibal-killers are concerned, we are probably in for an international feast.

Worldwide instances

In 1992 twenty-three old Mark Heggie drank his girlfriend's blood in north London, and joined John George Haigh (see page 154) on the short list of famous British vampires. Three years earlier, a young Australian woman named Tracey

Wigginton murdered a man in Brisbane with the same end in mind. Friends said how certain she was of her need for blood. In the Brazilian city of Rio, Marcelo Costa de Andrade killed fourteen boys in the latter part of 1991. When arrested he said he had drunk their blood to inherit their youth and good looks.

The same year saw the trial of Egyptian-born Omeima Nelson. The twenty-four-year-old Omeima had only just married her victim, an American drug smuggler more than twice her age. She claimed he had sexually assaulted her, and that she had merely defended herself by stabbing him with a pair of scissors and beating him to death with an iron. The faint remains of her credibility leaked away when it transpired that she had butchered, cooked and eaten parts of the corpse.

Omeima's conversations with the authorities provided several versions of the event. She claimed she was a 'warm person who wouldn't hurt a mosquito', and told a probation officer that she 'could not even cut her own hair, much less someone who weighed 230 pounds'. She resolutely denied eating her husband, and claimed that someone was trying to frame her. The examining psychiatrists, on the other hand, were given a blow-by-blow account.

She had dressed in bright red – hat, high heels and lipstick – for the butchering, had vengefully castrated the late Mr Nelson, and had boiled away his fingerprints to avoid detection. She had cooked his ribs in barbecue sauce, 'just like in a restaurant' (see Askenasy, Bibliography).

History repeats itself

In 1999 Dorangel Vargas put Venezuelan cannibalism on the map. He was arrested when the San Cristobal police found human body parts strewn around his house. Inside, they found many more, prompting Vargas to a frank admission – 'Sure, I eat people' (see Anon, Bibliography). And he was more than willing to share the experience with reporters. He stressed the need to wash the meat (so as to avoid diseases), and to garnish it properly, too. He personally favoured thighs and calves, but could recommend tongue stew and eye soup. He had not eaten hands, feet or testicles, but had given some thought to doing so. Elderly meat was too tough, fat people too full of cholesterol.

Vargas would not confess to any killings, claiming that he was given corpses by various people, including the police. There was also a suggestion that human organ

Celebrity cannibal: family money helped keep Sagawa out of prison – and socially acceptable

traffickers had picked him out as a useful scapegoat. The local press, on the other hand, were full of claims that he murdered drifters with a metal bar.

Getting away with murder

The most famous modern cannibal from outside the Big Three is probably Issei Sagawa. The son of a wealthy Japanese industrialist, Sagawa enjoyed – and, despite his crime, continues to enjoy – virtual immunity from justice. His first brush with the law came in 1970s Tokyo, when he broke into a western female student's room. The incident was hushed up, and Sagawa was taken to a psychiatrist who pronounced him 'extremely dangerous'. In the event, his father either did not agree with the diagnosis or he refused to give it credence; he paid for his son to study in France, where western female students were thick on the ground.

Sagawa later said that he had been obsessed by cannibalism since childhood. On one occasion he blamed a childhood nightmare of being boiled in a pot for this obsession; on another, he put it down to a game frequently played with his uncle and father, in which he and his brother were carried off to provide an imaginary feast. He kept this cannibal fantasy fed with fairy stories and comics, turning it around so that he became the feaster, and settling on the primary object of his culinary desire – a large and beautiful western woman.

He found her in Paris: Renée Hartevelt was a tall blonde PhD student who spoke three languages and found the diminutive Sagawa intellectually interesting. He asked her to his apartment, gave her a book of poetry to read, and shot her in the back of the head for no other reason than he wanted to eat her. Over the next few days he did just that, eating some pieces raw, others fried with salt and pepper. 'Finally I was eating a beautiful white woman, and thought nothing was so delicious!' (see Maringale, Bibliography).

He bought two large suitcases, crammed what was left of Renée inside, and tried to dump them in the Bois de Boulogne. The sight of Sagawa lugging two heavy suitcases through a park was made yet more suspicious when he panicked, dropped the cases and ran off. A protruding hand and copious bloodstains persuaded witnesses to call the police.

At this point the Sagawa story becomes something more than the usual pathetic tale of a psychological inadequate and his tragic victims. The French police and judiciary listened to his story and, unlike their American compatriots on many similar occasions, decided Sagawa was mentally incompetent to stand trial. They put him in the Paul Guiraud asylum, and set about seeing if he could be cured. No, they decided, and shipped him home.

Sagawa was already a celebrity in his own country, having collaborated in a novel about his crime. The Japanese police wanted to charge him, but the French – perhaps fearing that they would look foolish – refused to pass on the evidence for the case. Sagawa's father persuaded the Japanese asylum to discharge him, and, a mere four years after killing Renée Hartevelt, Sagawa was back on the street.

He wrote more books on his experiences, became a media standby for other cannibal cases, contributed to porn magazines and began appearing in films which aped his own story. He wrote restaurant reviews and exhibited paintings, most of which featured large-buttocked blondes. Sagawa had achieved the seemingly impossible – he had made a lucrative career out of killing and eating an innocent young woman.

Sagawa was taken to a psychiatrist who pronounced him 'extremely dangerous'.

Cannibal books and movies

Following the latest cannibal trials on the news is all very well, but real life sometimes seems sadly lacking in drama. Reading or watching a well-constructed account, leavened perhaps with the odd fictional embellishment or two, can be much more satisfying. And why, come to that, bother with real people or situations? Wholly fictional stories are so much neater, so much better geared to what the listener, watcher and buyer really want.

Musical cannibalism

Take Sweeney Todd, the 'demon barber of Fleet Street'. He's been around so long, in so many media incarnations, that few people can remember – if they ever knew – whether the original character was fact, part-fact or wholly fictional. Sweeney was a Victorian creation, a barber who cut more than his customers' hair, and passed on the corpses to the bakery next door, where Mrs Lovatt used them in her delicious pies. The original British version was written by Tom Prest under the title *The String of Pearls*, but the story had its origins as far back as fifteenth-century France. If based on fact – if some Parisian barber was indeed caught committing such a crime – then the evidence has long been lost.

Fact or fiction, Sweeney and his French forbear were eminently feasible, and like all such creations have enjoyed a long artistic shelf-life. The story has gone through many variations – the swivelling barber's chair, for example, which tipped the fresh corpse into the cellar beneath – and many media. A film, *Sweeney Todd, Demon Barber of Fleet Street*, was made in 1936, starring the aptly-named Tod Slaughter. Forty years later the story even begat the musical *Sweeney Todd*.

Cookery books

Cannibalism's appearance in stories goes back a lot further than the fifteenth century – Greek myths and legends, for example, are full of gods and people eating human flesh. Ovid, Seneca and Hesiod all have uplifting cannibal stories to tell, like Ovid's tale of two sisters in *Metamorphoses*. Tereus rapes his sister-in-law Philomena, then cuts off her hands and tongue to stop her revealing his name. She eventually works out a way of telling her sister Procne, who wreaks revenge on Tereus by dishing up their son for his dinner.

Over the centuries most literary luminaries had a few words to say. Shakespeare re-wrote Ovid's story as *Titus Andronicus*, and used Othello's encounter with cannibals to give him a bit of glamour. Dante's *Inferno* has a suitably gory piece of survival cannibalism, and Voltaire's *Candide* features a few buttock-eating Turks. Few went as far as Jonathan Swift, whose *Modest Proposal* suggested cannibalism as the solution to Irish poverty. 'I have been assured by a very knowing American of my acquaintance in London, that a young and healthy child

well nursed is at a year old a most delicious, nourishing and wholesome food, whether stewed, roasted, baked or boiled, and I make no doubt that it will equally serve in a fricassee, or a ragout.' Swift is being satirical, and we can only hope that Ireland's English landlords realized as much.

> Greek myths and legends...are full of gods and people eating human flesh. Ovid, Seneca and Hesiod all have cannibal stories to tell.

In Victorian times both Edgar Allan Poe and Mark Twain tried variations on the drawing-lots-for-dinner theme. Poe set his *Narrative of A. Gordon Pym* of Nantucket on a whaler, Twain's *Cannibalism in the Cars* takes place on a snowbound train in the American West. Herman Melville explored the subject in several projects. In his semi-autobiographical novel *Typee,* he cast a non-judgemental eye over the cannibalistic culture of the Marquesas

Islands, while the better-known *Moby Dick* features the character of Queequeg, a thoroughly civilized cannibal. Both Flaubert's *Salammbo* and Tolstoy's *Resurrection* contain scenes of cannibalism; the former, set in a fictional antiquity, seems to revel in blood and entrails.

The first famous science fiction novel with a cannibalistic theme was H.G. Wells' *The Time Machine*. A Victorian scientist travels into the future, where he finds an apparently idyllic, workless society. A little more investigation reveals that humanity has evolved in two separate directions – the beautiful creatures that our scientist has met on the surface, and the hairy monsters beneath. The former have no work because they are food-in-waiting, raised and fed by the monsters for eventual consumption.

Twentieth-century authors picked at the subject, and sometimes swallowed it whole. In Norman Mailer's *An American Dream* one character fantasizes about sharing his wife, food-wise, with his maid. In the same author's *The Presidential Papers,* he lists cannibalism among the topics 'a president ought to consider, and rarely does.' The plot of Tennessee Williams' *Suddenly Last Summer* revolves around one traumatic incident, in which a woman sees her cousin attacked and devoured by a band of street children.

Brett Easton Ellis blended sexual psychopathy and cannibalism to devastating – some thought disgusting – effect in *American Psycho*. His central character Patrick Bateman is a Kemper or Dahmer with lots of money and a swish apartment. Thomas Harris went even further, fashioning a cannibal anti-hero out of Hannibal Lecter, who starred in the series of novels which begin with *Red Dragon*. 'Hannibal the Cannibal', however, was not so much a literary character as a cinematic icon.

Eating for the camera

H.G. Wells' *The Time Machine* was first filmed in 1960, with Roy Taylor as the scientist; inferior re-makes followed in 1978 and 2002. The cannibalism was suggested rather than shown, presumably on grounds of taste. There are no obvious technical problems bringing morsels of human flesh to the screen, though film-makers have faced something of a challenge in the re-creation of convincing half-eaten corpses. Needless to say, many have pulled it off. Would that such dedication and expertise could be put to socially useful purposes.

The various types of cannibalism have all been brought to the silver screen. Cultural cannibalism has usually been relegated to the status of exotic backdrop – jungle drums and fear of the cooking pot in Hollywood's heyday, freaked-out-teens-in-Third-World-gap-year-horror in more recent times. The Mangeromas and

Bafum-Bansaws might be photogenic, sexy and violent as hell, but who would George Clooney and Nicole Kidman get to play?

Survival cannibalism has had a better deal. There have been excellent documentaries on the Donner party and Franklin Expedition. The former has inspired at least one, somewhat tepid movie – *Donner Pass: The Road to Survival* (1984). *Ravenous* (1999), a less family-oriented Western, seemed to pick and mix its plotlines, with less than devastating effect, from the Donner tragedy and Alferd Packer case. The latter also spawned an eponymous musical film, which one reviewer described as '*Cannibal Apocalypse* meets *Oklahoma*' (see Brottman, Bibliography). This Pythonesque gorefest with songs recounts Packer's own self-serving version of what happened in the wilderness.

The most serious of the survival cannibalism movies is *Alive!* (1993), the story of the Uruguayan rugby tour stranded in the Andes. Taken from Piers Paul Read's excellent book of the same name, it evokes all of the drama of the real event, and sometimes a little bit more. The cannibalism is taken seriously, but its depiction is very subdued, perhaps out of consideration for the relatives of those who were eaten. The mountains are far too beautiful, the scene around the stranded plane far too sanitized, but the overall effect is absorbing, particularly for those who do not know the outcome.

Cannibal biopics

The lives and times of real-life cannibal-

killers have continued to interest film-makers, for both good reasons and bad. Their careers undoubtedly raise real questions about the way individuals function in modern society, with the added bonus of shocks and plenty of gore.

Taken in chronological order – the cannibals, not the films – *Blood Clan* (1991) tells the story of Katy Beane, daughter of Sawney Beane and alleged survivor of the family's mass execution. The film-makers' research must have been amazingly thorough, because no one else has ever discovered a survivor. She ends up in Canada, and people start to go missing, etc.

Jeremiah Johnson, who gave his name to the film *Jeremiah Johnson* (1972) certainly existed, but was probably less ecologically-fixated than the character played by Robert Redford. Director (Sydney Pollack) and star agonized about Johnson's Indian-killing and the reasons for it – it just was not on in the early 1970s to cast Native Americans as savage murderers or launch genocidal campaigns against them. The screenplay solved the problem quite

In Norman Mailer's *An American Dream*, one character fantasizes about sharing his wife, food-wise, with his maid.

neatly: Johnson escorts a US cavalry mercy mission through an Indian burial ground, and this upsets the Indians so much that they kill his wife and child. Cue 'Death Wish in the Mountains'. The liver-eating is kept to a minimum.

At least two of the notorious German cannibals of the post-World War One period made it to the silver screen. Two films follow Fritz Haarmann's exploits – Uli Lommel's *Zaerlichkeit Der Voelfe* (Tenderness of Wolves) (1973) and Romuald Karmaker's *Totmacher* (Deathmaker) (1995), which is based on Haarmann's interrogations. John Zuri's *The Mad Butcher* (1972) is a looser homage, set in Vienna and involving sausage-making. The best-ever film about a cannibal – 'poetic, compassionate and chilling' (see Craddock, Bibliography) according to one reviewer – is probably Fritz Lang's classic art movie *M* (1931), in which Peter Lorre plays Peter Kurten, the Düsseldorf Vampire. None of these films features much in the way of chomping.

Ed Gein's crimes have almost spawned a film industry of their own. Antony Perkins' character in *Psycho* (1960) was clearly influenced by Gein's murderous mother-fixation, while *Three on a Meat-hook* (1972) and the films in *The Texas Chainsaw Massacre* (1974) series make full use of the props associated with him – the donning of human skin, the furniture and ornaments constructed from body parts. *Deranged* (1974) is truer to the actual story, and manages to inject a little black humour between blood-showers. *The Silence of the Lambs* (1991) made secondary use of Gein, employing signature elements of his story to pad out the secondary character, Buffalo Bill.

Of the more recent cannibal-killers, only Issei Sagawa, Jeffrey Dahmer and Andrei Chikatilo have so far made the translation to celluloid. Sagawa has involved himself in several cinematic versions of his crime, and continues to profit from it as a result. Dahmer's story is given an airing in David R. Bowen's *The Secret Life* (1993), but the cannibalistic element is largely ignored. *Citizen X* (1995), Chris Gerolmo's account of Chikatilo's criminal career goes even further, omitting the cannibalism altogether.

There is clearly scope for more. The Countess Bathory's story has everything the slasher genre could want, and only one location to pay for. Kemper, Heidnik, Kroll and the rest are waiting in the cinematic wings. And one cannot help thinking that Anna Zimmerman would make a great character for a soap.

That is entertainment?

Movies about wholly fictional cannibals

Jeremiah Johnson's story was slightly sanitized by Hollywood when it hit the silver screen but is a true tale

and cannibalism are generally less interesting. They fall into much the same genres as any other films – epics of survival, contemporary slasher/horror flicks, sci-fi movies, satires of modern life, police procedurals.

Five Came Back (1939), the story of a small group who survive a plane crash in the South American jungle, was made thirty-three years before the Uruguayan rugby players were forced to do it for real. Many other movies have followed the same basic pattern, albeit with variations. In *The Severed Arm* (1973), a group facing starvation draw lots to decide whose arm will be amputated to feed them. All are rescued soon after the meal, and go their separate ways. But the newly one-armed man proves a sore loser.

Slasher movies frequently use cannibalism as a gore-escalator, but rarely

The infamous film *The Silence of the Lambs*: chianti and fava beans will never be seen in the same light again

have anything to say. Their titles are frequently the best thing about them – who could resist *Crazy Fat Ethel II* (1985), *Bloodsucking Pharaohs of Pittsburg* (1990) or *Rabid Grannies* (1989)? *The Texas Chainsaw Massacre* series has its fans, but then so does Morris dancing. One sub-genre that deserves mentioning uses the Sweeney Todd template. *Auntie Lee's Meat Pies* (1992) has five nieces – four of them played by Playboy bunnies – enticing young males into providing the mince, while the *The Untold Story: Human Meat Roast Pork Buns* (1993) moves much the same plot to pre-return Hong Kong.

Anything goes in sci-fi, and that includes cannibalism. *Alien Prey* (1983) begins with lesbians making love, but then has them eaten by an alien. *Adrenalin: Fear the Rush* (1996) uses a plague to create an army of cannibal-killers; *Bad Taste* (1988) features alien fast food merchants who fasten on Earth as a source of meat. *Soylent Green* (1973) has much the same idea, but without the aliens, and only applied to the elderly. Even older, more ambitious, and now something of a cult classic, *Night of the Living Dead* (1968) has radiation-resurrected stiffs with a taste for human flesh.

Cannibalism is used to make a point in several satirical explorations of modern life. In *Weekend* (1967) Jean-Luc Godard offers it up as the perfect ending to his Parisian couple's trip through bourgeois emptiness; in *The Thief, The Cook, His Wife and Her Lover* (1990) Peter Greenaway has the heroine force-feed her lover to her husband with a choke-on-this smile. *Eating Raoul* (1982) has a young couple investing an upstairs neighbour's corpse in their new restaurant; *Delicatessen* (1992) is a French comedy built around a futuristic Sweeney Todd. *Fried Green Tomatoes* (1991) is that rare thing indeed, a movie that makes you feel glad that someone's been eaten.

The final mention must go to *The Silence of The Lambs* (1991), the movie which brought cinematic cannibalism into the mainstream. As the appalling Hannibal Lecter, Anthony Hopkins conjures up the cannibal of our dreams, articulate, philosophical, alluringly scary. Thankfully he bears no resemblance to any real cannibal-killer, living or dead.

7: Looking to the Future

There are two Charlton Heston movies which end with our hero realizing that things are far, far worse than he could ever have imagined. In both cases he gasps out 'Oh my God!' or something similar, and sinks, at least metaphorically, to his knees. One of these movies is *Planet of the Apes*, which ends with Chuck's realization that he has been travelling in time rather than space, and that the planet of the apes is Earth. The other is *Soylent Green*, which ends with him finding out that the miracle foodstuff of the title is in fact made from America's senior citizens.

> **On the face of it, desperation cannibalism seems ripe for extinction. For one thing, the potential for getting lost at sea or on land has definitely shrunk. Few parts of the world remain either unexplored or beyond the reach of modern communications technology.**

Has the human race put cannibalism firmly behind it, creating a global taboo which only a few crazies will seek to break? Or does the current situation merely reflect a particular set of circumstances hostile to the habit, circumstances which could well disappear? Could human flesh and blood be the taste of the not-so-distant future?

Getting desperate

On the face of it, desperation cannibalism seems ripe for extinction. For one thing, the potential for getting lost at sea or on land has definitely shrunk. Few parts of the world remain either unexplored or beyond the reach of modern communications technology. These days the stranded sailors would be texting their position to all and sundry, and any rugby teams lost in the Andes who could not get a signal would still be visible to heat-seeking satellites. These days, it takes a real effort to get lost.

The same global reach applies to famines. The world currently creates enough food for all its people, and though skewed distribution means that many still go hungry, the media and charity organizations usually ensure that areas facing famine receive emergency relief. People – and especially children – do die in unforgivable numbers, but some sort of assistance is usually forthcoming, the sort of assistance that was unavailable to victims in earlier centuries. Perhaps for this reason, perhaps for others, cannibalism has rarely been mentioned in connection with the famines which have haunted Africa over the last twenty years. It might, in a ghoulish sort of way, be interesting to see the reaction of Western donors if it were. Would they recognize it as

a sign of utter desperation, or recoil in horror and self-righteously turn their backs?

We may yet get the chance to find out. There is now general agreement – always excluding the oil industry glitterati currently in charge of the US government – that global warming has been under way for some time, and is likely to accelerate over the coming decades. The effects are bound to be serious, but just how serious, and just how quickly they will be felt, remain to be seen. The most recent signs are on the scary side.

The effects themselves – the general warming, shift of climatic patterns, rising sea levels, etc – may benefit some areas in the long run, but they will certainly make life much harder in others, and everywhere will see some kind of economic shake-up. Some things seem more certain than others. Large areas of Africa will get hotter and drier; grasslands will turn to semi-deserts, semi-deserts to deserts. Food production is likely to fall, let alone keep pace with a rising population. Famines will last longer and become yet more serious, at a time when the rest of the world is facing growing food troubles of its own. Widespread cannibalism is a distinct possibility.

Many African countries are already in serious economic difficulty, and there are few signs that those who can make the necessary sacrifices – the richer countries and African elites – are prepared to do so. This general malaise has already induced a plethora of interminable civil wars, and seems likely to induce more. Cultural cannibalism is far from a distant memory in many parts of the continent, and the likelihood of it surfacing in such future wars – as it already has in Sierra Leone, Liberia, Congo and Rwanda – seems extremely high.

Getting depraved

Cannibalism is not against the law in many countries – Germany, to take just one example – but procuring the food almost always involves some sort of illegal act, from pilfering blood samples to murder. There will always be some people sufficiently motivated to commit such crimes, but will the number rise significantly in the years to come? There are reasons for thinking it will.

There is little agreement on what turns people into cannibal-killers. Some favour nature as an explanation – that the person in question is genetically pre-disposed to such acts. Others favour nurture: the home environment, school environment, the

Many of the cannibal killers in this book, for example, had punitive fathers and over-bearing mothers. None received the sort of love necessary for building self-esteem.

social environment as a whole – they all impact on individuals, pushing some in more destructive directions than others. Many of the cannibal-killers in this book, for example, had punitive fathers and over-protective or over-bearing mothers. None received the sort of love necessary for building self-esteem. And it is of course probable that nature and nurture reinforce each other; that a harmful environment will bring out what the good environment leaves buried.

If some people are genetically inclined towards violence in general and cannibalism in particular, there seems no reason why their number should be increasing. If nurture plays a greater role in producing such people, then we must look at Western social norms – the ones that cultural globalization are exporting to the rest of the world – and ask the relevant questions. Are more children being raised by abusive parents? Are human relations in general more abusive? Does society as a whole tolerate higher levels of bad behaviour among its citizens?

Famines [in Africa] will last longer and become yet more serious, at a time when the rest of the world is facing growing food troubles of its own. Widespread cannibalism is a distinct possibility.

Sadly, the answer to these questions seems to be 'yes'. As if to prove as much, the incidence and harshness of violent crime are both inexorably rising. The number of American murders, for example, tripled between the 1960s and 1990s. More and more people are killing strangers, and revealing their twisted psyches in the way that they do it. It seems more than likely that a growing number will be twisted in the direction of cannibalism.

Cultural revival?

At least cultural cannibalism seems unripe for revival. As their birth-rates decline and their old live longer, many Western societies are succumbing to pensions crises, but no political parties have, as yet, championed the *Soylent Green* model as a solution. A combination of ridding the world of conflict and a cure for cancer might get us there, but the PR and marketing would have to be very carefully designed. Big Macs made of real Scotsmen are, thankfully, still some way off.

Bibliography

Books

1) Abd al-Latif *Relation de l'Egypte par Abd Allatif, Médecin arabe de Bagdad* (Paris, 1810) translated by Reay Tannahill

2) Anon *Cannibals and Evil Cult Killers* (London, Time Warner, 2005)

3) Arens, William *Man-Eating Myth: Anthropology and Anthropophagy* (New York, Oxford University Press, 1980)1) Askenasy, Hans *Cannibalism from Sacrifice to Survival* (New York, Prometheus Books, 1994)

4) Bentley, Rev. W. Holman *Pioneering on the Congo* (RTS, 1900)

5) Chong, Key Ray *Cannibalism in China* (Longwood Academic, 1990)

6) Conklin, Beth A. *Consuming Grief* (University of Texas Press, 2001)

7) Elkin A.P. *The Australian Aborigines* (Angus & Robertson, 1938)

8) Endicott, William *Wrecked among Cannibals in the Fijis* (Salem, Marine Research Society, 1923)

9) Figes, Orlando *A People's Tragedy: The Russian Revolution 1891-1924* (London, Pimlico, 1996)

10) Greig, Charlotte *Evil Serial Killers* (London, Arcturus, 2005)

11) Hogg, Gary *Cannibalism and Human Sacrifice* (London, Robert Hale, 1958)

12) Jacob, H.E. *Six Thousand Years of Bread: Its Holy and Unholy history* (New York, 1944)

13) James, E.O. *Origins of Sacrifice* (John Murray, 1933)

14) Johnson, Captain Charles *A General History of the Lives and Adventures of the Most Famous Highwaymen, Murderers, Street-Robbers, etc* (London, J.Jameway, 1734)

15) Korn, Daniel; Radice, Mark & Hawes, Charlie *Cannibal: The History of the People-Eaters* (London, Channel 4 Books, 2001)

16) Krafft-Ebbing, Richard von *Aberrations of Sexual Life: The Psychopathia Sexualis* (London, Panther, 1965)

17) Lange, Algot *In the Amazon Jungle* (New York, Putnam, 1912)

18) Marriner, Brian *Cannibalism: The Last Taboo* (London, Arrow, 1992)

19) Martingale, Moira *Cannibal Killers* (New York, St Martin's, 1993)

20) Metraux, A *Easter Island* (Andre Deutsch, 1957)

21) Price, Merrall Llewelyn *Consuming Passions* (Routledge, 2003)

22) Read, Piers Paul *Alive!* (London, Avon, 1992)

23) Roscoe, John *The Bagesu and Other Tribes of the Uganda Protectorate* (The Royal Society, 1924)

24) St. Johnston, Alfred *Camping among Cannibals* (Macmillan, 1883)

25) Salisbury, Harrison E. *The 900 Days* (Pan, 2000)

26) Tannahill, Reay *Flesh and Blood: The History of the Cannibal Complex* (London, Abacus, 1996)

27) Thomas, Lowell *The Wreck of the Dumaru* (Doubleday, Doran & Company Inc, 1930)

28) Yi, Zheng *The Scarlet Memorial: Tales of Cannibalism in Modern China* (New York, Westview Press, 1998)

Articles

Article 1: Keenleyside, Anne, *et al* 'The final days of the Franklin Expedition: new skeletal evidence', Arctic – Journal of the *Arctic Institute of North America*, Vol 50, No.1 (University of Calgary, March 1997)

Article 2: *Memorandum to a Cannibal* on http://www.worldnetdaily.com/news/article

Article 3: www.cnn.com/2004/WORLD/europe/01/30/germany.cannibal/

Index

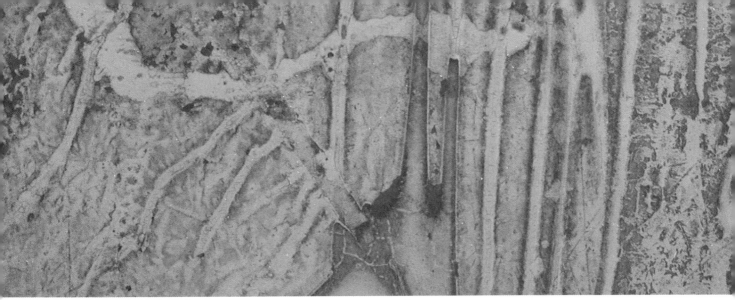

PICTURE LIST

Images reproduced on the following pages with the permission of the following:

Art Archive (Picture Desk):
2, 9, 13, 17, 18, 25, 35, 38, 43, 55, 115

Corbis:
15, 33, 46, 49, 67, 95, 125, 139, 145, 147, 159, 161, 182, 189

Empics:
109, 129, 131, 155, 163, 166, 167, 169, 170, 172, 174, 176, 186, 190, 192

Getty:
6–7, 10, 22, 37, 69, 70, 74–75, 86, 90, 92, 96, 101, 103, 105, 150, 152, 178, 180

Kobal (Art Archive):
198
Mary Evans:
29, 57, 116

Rex:
65, 79, 80, 113, 127, 137, 194, 200, 132

Topfoto:
21, 26, 59, 60, 119, 141, 143, 184